The
Welfare
of
Citizens

The Welfare of Citizens

Developing new social rights

**edited by
Anna Coote**

IPPR/Rivers Oram Press
London

I?PR

First published in 1992 by
Rivers Oram Press
144 Hemingford Road, London N1 1DE

Published in the USA by
Paul and Company
Post Office Box 442, Concord, MA 01742

Set in 9pt Sabon
and printed in Great Britain
by T.J. Press (Padstow) Ltd, Padstow, Cornwall

Cover/book design: Katherine Gutkind, Accent on type

British Library Cataloguing in Publication Data
A catalogue record for this book is available from the British Library

ISBN 1-85489-037-9
ISBN 1-85489-038-7 pbk

CONTENTS

ACKNOWLEDGEMENTS

I am indebted to all the authors for their invaluable, and largely unrewarded contributions; to Raymond Plant for inspiring this project in the first place, and to Tessa Harding for her moral and intellectual support in getting it off the ground. This project would not have been possible without the generous support of the Joseph Rowntree Foundation. Many thanks are also due to those who participated in preparatory seminars and meetings at IPPR, especially Nick Doyle, Fedelma Winkler, Ian Bynoe, Naomi Pfeffer, Karen Meador and Liz Wynn. For their help with the introduction, thanks to Donald Sassoon, David Miliband and James Cornford.

LIST OF CONTRIBUTORS

Raymond Plant is Professor of Politics at Southampton University. In 1990/1 he was Stanton Lecturer at Cambridge University and Sarum Lecturer at Oxford University. His books include *Hegel*; *Conservative Capitalism in Britain and the United States: A Critical Appraisal* (with K. Hoover); and *Modern Political Thought*.

Norman Lewis is Professor of Public Law at the Centre for Socio-Legal Studies, Sheffield University. His books include *The Noble Lie: The British Constitution and the Rule of Law*, and *Government by Moonlight: The Hybrid Parts of the State*.

Mary Seneviratne is a solicitor and a senior lecturer at the School of Financial and Legal Studies, Sheffield City Polytechnic.

Denis Galligan is Professor of Law at Southampton University and Professor at the University of Sydney. His books include *Discretionary Powers* and *Due Process and Fair Procedures* (forthcoming).

Nick Doyle is a Senior Researcher at the National Consumer Council. He is co-author of *Open to Complaints: Guidelines for Social Services Complaints Procedures*.

Tessa Harding is a Consultant at the National Institute for Social Work. She is author of *Great Expectations . . . and Spending on Social Services* and was formerly Project Leader of the Community Care Project at the National Council for Voluntary Organisations.

Jonathan Montgomery is a lecturer in law at Southampton University. He is co-author (with David Carson) of *Nursing and the Law*.

Nina Biehal is a research fellow at the Department of Adult Continuing Education at the University of Leeds and is a former social worker.

Mike Fisher is a lecturer in Applied Social Studies at the University of Bradford, jointly directing research programmes covering partnership approaches in child and community care. He is a former social worker.

Peter Marsh teaches and researches at the University of Sheffield, where he is Director of the Partnership Practice Programme.

Eric Sainsbury is Emeritus Professor of Social Administration at the University of Sheffield.

Wendy Thomson is Assistant Chief Executive at the London Borough of Islington, where she is responsible for policy development.

Priscilla Alderson is at the Social Science Research Unit, Institute of Education, University of London. Her research at the Community Paediatric Research Unit, Westminster Children's Hospital, was sponsored by the Leverhulme Trust. She is author of *Choosing for Children: Parents' Consent to Surgery*.

The Editor

Anna Coote is a Research Fellow of the Institute for Public Policy Research, where she is responsible for a project, funded by the Joseph Rowntree Foundation and others, to develop strategies for a modern welfare system. She is co-author of *The Family Way: A new approach to policy making* (with Harriet Harman and Patricia Hewitt, IPPR, 1990); and *Is Quality Good for You? A critical review of quality assurance in welfare services* (with Naomi Pfeffer, IPPR, 1991). Before joining IPPR she wrote and produced *Next Left*, a four-part documentary series on political ideas in Europe (Channel Four Television, 1989). She has been editor of *Diverse Reports*, a weekly current affairs series for Channel Four TV, Deputy Editor of the *New Statesman* and a freelance journalist and broadcaster. Her other books include *Power and Prejudice: Women and Politics* (with Polly Pattullo), *Sweet Freedom* (with Beatrix Campbell), *Women's Rights: A Practical Guide* (with Tess Gill) and *Civil Liberty: The NCCL Guide* (with Lawrence Grant). In 1991 she was appointed Senior Lecturer in the Department of Media and Communications at Goldsmiths College, University of London.

INTRODUCTION

Questions about the nature and purpose of Britain's welfare system have been more hotly contested during the 1980s and 1990s than at any time since the Beveridge Report was published fifty years ago. But as Left and Right have diverged in their views about the kind of system that is needed for the twenty-first century, the language has converged. There is now discussion of citizens' charters and citizens' rights across the political spectrum.

This volume is about citizens' rights to welfare services. It has been prepared by the Institute for Public Policy Research as part of a broader programme of work to develop strategies for a modern welfare system. The chapters which follow are an attempt to open up a new field of debate in British politics. In spite of all the talk about charters and rights, the philosophical and practical implications of developing social rights of citizenship have not yet been explored. We do not pretend to offer definitive answers, but hope to raise some pertinent questions and start some useful arguments. The work in this volume builds on four propositions about welfare rights, developed by Raymond Plant in Chapter 1.

The first is that, contrary to the claims of some prominent critics on the Right, there is no categorical difference between social and economic rights on the one hand, and civil and political rights on the other. The philosophical case for social rights, such as rights to health care and other welfare services, is no less plausible than the case for civil liberties, such as freedom from coercion or assault, and freedom of speech and assembly.

The second proposition is that social rights, to be anything other than a sham, must be enforceable by individual citizens.

The third is that the idea of enforceable social rights offers a new way of empowering citizens, different from the traditional models of empowerment favoured by the Right (market choices) and by the Left (democratic accountability). Social rights are not presented here as some kind of universal solution, overriding markets and democracy as a means of empowerment, but as an alternative – and possibly complementary – approach which deserves further investigation.

The fourth proposition is that social rights can be introduced through a range of mechanisms, to suit different services and different circumstances. It is neither necessary nor feasible to impose a total package at a single stroke, to apply uniformly across the field of welfare services. If individually enforceable rights are the goal, then that goal must be approached from a number of angles, across a wide terrain. The ground must be tested thoroughly at each point, and strategies tried and adapted, according to experience. What works in one kind of service may not work in another; what works in the longer term may not work immediately, but may require an interim or transitional strategy. None of this makes for a neat thesis or a clean-cut argument. But it is the only way to proceed if our purpose is practical rather than polemical.

It would be impossible in one volume to cover all the ground. We examine two strategies for introducing social rights, which are separate but compatible. One, proposed by Norman Lewis and Mary Seneviratne, is to enact a Social Charter for the United Kingdom, based on international treaties to which the UK is already committed. This would be concerned with substantive issues such as medical care, social security and housing. It would be a statement of values and aspirations, rather than a set of directly enforceable individual rights.

The second strategy, which we consider in more detail, is to develop procedural rights, designed to suit different welfare services. These are rights not to actual services or benefits, but to the fair treatment of individuals as they come into contact (or try to come into contact) with service providers. They could be enforced, through a range of possible mechanisms, by the individuals themselves. They would be underpinned by the values expressed in the Social Charter.

We have brought together lawyers and social policy analysts to explore the theme of procedural rights. The principles of procedural fairness are set out by Denis Galligan and further expounded, with particular reference to community care, by Nick Doyle and Tessa Harding. Jonathan Montgomery considers the possibilities and problems of establishing rights to health and to health care. Nina Biehal and others draw on their detailed study of relations between social workers and their clients to develop proposals for users' rights to fair treatment in this field.

The last two chapters in this volume open the debate in two further directions. Wendy Thomson cautions that nationally legislated rights will not be sufficient to empower users of welfare services. She argues for people's direct involvement, describing work on service contracts being implemented in local authorities: agreements negotiated locally and bound by guarantees, backed by procedures for complaint and redress. Priscilla Alderson raises the question of who should enjoy social rights and why. She examines children's rights to consent, their developing competence and their complex and shifting status in society.

Rights move on to the agenda

When we began work on these chapters, political discussion about citizens' rights was developing on two fronts. There was growing interest, on the one hand, in a Bill of Rights and a written constitution for the United Kingdom. This had been a preoccupation of the centre parties for some time, and gradually spread to the Left during the years in which Margaret Thatcher's Conservatives held an irresistible majority in Parliament. The formation of Charter 88, the campaign for electoral and constitutional reform, was one manifestation of this trend. The development at the IPPR of a draft Constitution of the United Kingdom, including a Bill of Rights, was another. The Labour Party's abandonment of its opposition to a Bill of Rights and its establishment in 1991 of the Plant Commission to examine electoral reform, was yet another.

Meanwhile in the European Community, social rights were moving up the political agenda as member governments prepared their electorates for a single market and monetary union. EC President Jacques Delors's speech to the Trades Union Congress at Bournemouth in 1989 began to persuade the British labour movement that a European Social Charter, conferring rights upon individuals and enshrined in EC law, could be the best hope for protecting the living standards of working people. In Maastricht in 1991 it was, interestingly, this social dimension of European unity, more than any monetary question, which proved the sticking point for John Major. As the gap continued to narrow between the economic policies of Left and Right, welfare policies looked set to be a key site of political dispute for the remainder of the century. A significant part of the dispute seemed likely to turn on the question of whether health and social services and benefits were to be certain rights or uncertain privileges – and for whom.

The stand-off at Maastricht was a sign of things to come, but the depth of disagreement was temporarily camouflaged. As the 1980s gave way to the 1990s and Margaret Thatcher to John Major, Left and Right had indeed come to agree on some important points of welfare policy. They now agreed (broadly) that costs of services should be contained, that services should be more flexible to meet individual needs, and that individuals should have more say in how their needs were met. They agreed, too, that services should be specified and standards set, and that if things went wrong users should be able to complain and seek redress. More significantly, the Left had come around to the view that direct state provision of services was not always the best guarantee of quality, while the Right had had to admit that privatisation was not either, and that some services should continue to be provided by public agencies.

For a while it seemed that Government and Opposition were simply vying with each other to show who would do more to promote the rights of individual citizens to high-quality public services. In June 1991, Labour brought out its own 'Citizen's Charter' just days before the Conservative Government published a White Paper by the same name. Labour's Charter declared that 'consumers need rights to protect themselves and to buttress their purchasing power' and 'as citizens, they need powers to have those rights enforced.' The Conservatives' Charter claimed to be 'a testament of our belief in people's right to be informed and choose for themselves' and promised to publish 'a new standard for the delivery of quality in public services.'

On closer inspection, however, the two documents could be seen to carry quite different messages. Labour's Charter promised to give 'consumers and citizens nine practical rights in their dealings with companies, public bodies and central and local government'. These were not only rights to choice, quality, swift and fair redress, a say in decisionmaking and information, but also rights to safety, equal treatment, citizen's action and advocacy. The Conservatives' Charter promised to publish performance targets and information on standards achieved, and to introduce more effective complaints procedures, tougher inspectorates and better redress for the citizen, but spoke little of rights and made several major undertakings which had nothing to do with them at all: more privatisation, wider competition, further contracting out and more performance-related pay.

As this comparison suggests, Left and Right have divergent views about how services should be delivered. This springs from a more fundamental conflict – about what a welfare system is for and what it should seek to achieve. And this in turn reflects profoundly different ideas about equality, individual empowerment and collective action.

On the Left there is a widely held belief that public policy should aim to promote equal opportunity in the broad sense of providing everyone with an equal chance in life. This is based on an understanding that people do not start out on the proverbial 'level playing field': many have disadvantages, of which some are constructed and avoidable, while others are inherent or insuperable. Welfare policies should therefore aim to minimise the avoidable disadvantages and compensate for the others, in order to equalise the 'life chances' of all. The idea of 'life chances' is closely linked to the idea of individual empowerment as a requirement of citizenship. Citizenship entails being able to participate in society, to enjoy its fruits and to fulfil one's own potential, and it follows that each individual citizen must be equally able (or 'empowered') to do so. This suggests two things: first, that all individuals must have equal access to education, health care and other services necessary to give them an equal chance in life. Second, no-one should be subject to unfair discrimination. As the IPPR has argued elsewhere, there should be added to existing legislation against sex and race discrimination, a law against discrimination on grounds of disability. A substantial lobby for such a law had developed by the early 1990s, chiefly among groups of disabled people. They were seeking a model of welfare built not on need and philanthropy, but on *equal citizenship* as a means to self-determination. This view has been making an increasing impression on the Left's thinking about welfare.

The Right has another view. While John Major's Citizen's Charter insists 'that essential services – such as education and health – must be available to all, irrespective of means', the driving force behind the Right's policy-making is a commitment to *individual choice* as a means to self-determination. Inequality is a fair price to pay for freedom to choose. The Right believes that welfare policies should promote choice as far as possible, and provide a safety net for those who are beyond choosing to help themselves. A safety net is only equitable insofar as it catches all those who fall into it. It does nothing about the fact that some are more likely than others to lose their footing. The Right accepts the idea of citizens having equal rights but assumes a level playing field' and fails to acknowledge that citizens with unequal power may enforce rights in ways that compound existing inequalities. The Right sees the power of the state (or at least that of some state agencies) as being a major barrier to individual empowerment through choice. Free choice in the market place is seen as the most effective way of empowering individuals. Competition is the surest guarantee of choice, and the state should step in only where strictly necessary. If the market fails to provide competition, the preferred solution is to graft market features on to public agencies, as a means of promoting and protecting choice. The Conservative Government has been committed to restraining public expenditure and introducing market mechanisms into public services, not least because it believes that these are the best means of curbing the power of providers in what Margaret Thatcher and others have disparaged as the 'nanny state', spoon-feeding an increasingly dependent populace. There is no acknowledgement that the individual might require protection from unfettered market forces. The Government's Charter, unlike Labour's, makes no mention of individuals' rights in relation to private companies.

There is room for philanthropy in this view of the world, which acknowledges that the poor and needy are still with us and must be helped - preferably by individual volunteers and independent charities. There is little room, however, for collective action by citizens, either through the state as a collective mechanism, or when citizens are organised in groups which might challenge the power of employers or Government. Individual empowerment is desirable, but group empowerment is not.

The right-wing think tank, the Adam Smith Institute, which has played a key role in John Major's Citizen's Charter initiative, professes to be in favour of 'consulting' the public on the shape of public services. But ASI Director Madsen Pirie has made clear his distaste for any public participation in decision-making through neighbourhood forums or other public meetings. The kind of consultation he has in mind is to hire a polling organisation to carry out market research. This avoids any danger of individuals getting together as groups of citizens, or any obligation to enter into a dialogue or to negotiate with them. It keeps power in the hands of the body commissioning the research, which remains free to formulate the questions, interpret the answers and decide what to do about the results. Pirie and others would argue that groups are never representative of the 'public', and they have a point; in their view, this justifies an absence of dialogue between the state and the public, except through ballot box or opinion survey.

In effect, there is no distinction on the Right between the concept of the individual-to-be-empowered and concept of the individual consumer; 'citizen's rights' are simply about individuals having the right to make or not to make a transaction or receive a service, and to complain and seek redress if the goods or services are substandard.

The Left's thinking on collectivism has been more troubled – not least because it has always harboured a complex and sometimes contradictory combination of views. Since the early 1980s it has been reconsidering some of its customary commitments – particularly those concerning the 'scientific' welfarism inherited from the Webbs, the extent of trade union power, and the size of the state. At the same time it has had to defend, under heavy bombardment, some of its dearest ideals: public provision of public services as the most effective way of meeting public need; strong local democracy; the legitimacy of collective action by workers in trade unions, and by groups speaking for different localities and sections of the community. In the course of a decade, something of a transformation has taken place in the way the Left thinks about collectivism. This can be seen in the contrast between campaigns to defend public sector 'jobs and services' (in that order), and to restore public ownership, which preoccupied the Left in the early 1980s, and the Left's growing commitment in the early 1990s to 'quality' services. Locally negotiated service agreements described by Wendy Thomson, are about giving local people a voice in planning local services. Implicitly, they challenge the authority of scientific welfarism as well as the power of local authorities and public sector unions to determine how needs are met and services delivered. In this context, the idea of introducing individually enforceable welfare rights is part of a broader move to effect a shift in the culture of welfare by changing the way people think about it – from something which belongs to politicians, professionals and other experts, to something which belongs to the people for whom it is intended. Rights are not just for individuals as consumers; they are part of a package which also includes – crucially –

measures to strengthen the participation of citizens in defining welfare needs and planning services to meet those needs. Labour's Citizen's Charter pledges, for example, to 'encourage the development of local independent user and consumer groups', and to encourage local authorities 'to continue their political and financial support for voluntary community and self-help organisations'. These measures will need to address the problem that some groups are unrepresentative and many individuals are unable or unwilling to participate.

The status of social rights

Left and Right continue to talk about rights in relation to welfare and other public services: they use the same language, but with different meanings, as we have seen. Meanwhile very little has been said on either side about the status of these 'rights', and how, if at all, they might be enforced.

Some controversial questions arise. Should social and economic rights have the same status as civil and political rights? Which rights should be enforceable by individuals? By what means should rights be enforced? Will lawyers gain much and the public little? Will legal rights weaken democracy? Should groups have rights as well as individuals? What balance should be sought between nationally determined rights and local autonomy? Should any categories of people be excluded from enjoyment of rights?

Raymond Plant refutes the claim of critics on the Right that social rights cannot be enforceable in law because they imply a claim on resources – by pointing out that all rights require resources if they are to be enforced. He argues that liberty depends not simply on the absence of coercion, but on what we are able to do if we are not coerced, and that 'positive' (social) rights are therefore no less important than 'negative' (civil) rights such as freedom of speech and movement, because they can guarantee the abilities which make liberty worthwhile. If that is the case, does it necessarily follow that social rights should have the same constitutional status as civil rights? For those who support a Bill of Rights, especially one that is entrenched against simple majority votes in Parliament, this becomes an especially salient question. Should social rights be established in UK law? Should they be entrenched? Having established a philosophical case for social rights, Plant suggests a strategic approach to determining their status: 'rights should be looked at very carefully on a case-by-case basis to see how far they can be taken.'

Norman Lewis and Mary Seneviratne propose that certain social rights should be incorporated into UK law in the form of a Social Charter. They have produced their own draft charter, but make it clear that this detail is provided to open, rather than close, debate about what rights should be included and how each clause should be worded. (We pursue the debate within this volume:

Jonathan Montgomery proposes in Chapter 5 an alternative, draft clause on health.)

The kind of Social Charter proposed here is quite different from the Citizen's Charters of the Conservative Government or of the Labour Party. The latter deal with procedures; the former with substantive issues – for example, the promotion of health, provision of medical care, social security, legal and social protection of family life; social and economic protection for mothers and children, and for elderly people. Furthermore, the Lewis and Seneviratne Charter is significantly different from the draft Bill of Rights published by IPPR in 1990. The latter, which deals with civil and political rights, is drafted in terms of rights residing in individuals (for example, 'Everyone has the right. . . .') The former, which deals with social and economic rights, is drafted in terms of duties incumbent on the Government (for example, 'The Government undertakes to ensure. . . .') Furthermore, Lewis and Seneviratne do not suggest that their Social Charter be entrenched, while the IPPR's Bill of Rights is intended to be so. They propose that the Social Charter be introduced by an ordinary Act of Parliament; future legislation could revoke or derogate from it. It is intended essentially as a statement of principles, to express the values and aspirations of parliament, and to act as a guide for interpreting existing laws and regulations and for formulating legislation in the future.

There are two main reasons why the IPPR supports such a distinction between categories of rights – both are contentious. The first is based on the view that in a democracy civil liberties deserve a different constitutional status from social rights. The argument, put crudely, is that if all individuals in a society were comfortably housed and enjoyed reasonable standards of health care, education and social insurance, but had no civil rights, that society would offer them no constitutional means of winning the rights they lacked. By contrast, a society in which individuals enjoyed the right to vote, and freedoms of speech, assembly, movement and so forth, would hold out the possibility of winning social rights through the democratic process. Civil rights can thus be seen as a means of achieving social rights. Social rights may be necessary for the just enforcement of existing civil rights (since abilities make liberties worthwhile), but on their own they cannot be a means of achieving civil rights. And indeed, without civil rights, social rights are almost certainly unenforceable and therefore meaningless. On this practical ground, therefore, at this stage, there is a stronger case for entrenching civil rights than social rights.

The second, more pragmatic reason is that, for rights to be workable in practice they must be politically viable: there must be some degree of consensus about their desirability to support their enforcement. Broad support may be developing within the parties of Left and Centre in favour of a Bill of Rights dealing with civil and political liberties, but there is not yet evidence of equivalent political support for treating social and economic rights in the same manner, within UK law. After all, Britain is a novice in this field: unlike the US and most of its EC and Commonwealth partners, it has no experience of written constitutional rights. It, would, therefore seem sensible to proceed in stages on this front: to build a framework of social rights gradually, testing the impact of new measures on existing institutions and on public opinion. Lewis and Seneviratne set out proposals for implementing the Social Charter, based on lessons learned from the Council of Europe, on whose charter (subscribed by the UK) much of their draft is based. A great deal will depend on how effective the means of implementation turn out to be, and how, in practice, they can be improved as time goes by.

Such a Charter, though not directly enforceable by individuals, should nevertheless provide a supportive environment for the procedures described by Denis Galligan and others, in which individuals are intended to have some enforceable rights. There are three main reasons why we have chosen to concentrate on procedural as opposed to substantive rights. All are pragmatic. The first is that, although procedures do cost money, they do not have the same implications for resource allocation as do substantive rights. It is almost certainly easier to predict and control the costs of enforcing fair procedures, whereas the introduction of enforceable rights to services and benefits would imply unpredictable and open-ended demands on public funds.

The second reason is linked to the first. Claims by individuals to enforce rights will doubtless lead to rulings by judicial bodies which affect the way national or local government conducts its business. In the UK, where there is little in the way of an established tradition of courts interfering with the executive, any such interference is a matter of high political sensitivity. But where the rights are procedural rather than substantive, the courts or tribunals would be more likely to intervene at a relatively low level – on detail rather than on major policy issues.

The third reason is that procedural rights to welfare are in a sense a hybrid between civil and social rights. As Denis Galligan points out, there are certain basic ideas about procedural fairness which are already well developed in UK law. These can be summarised as follows: individuals should be heard before a decision is made concerning them; there should be no bias on the part of the decision-maker; people should be treated with equality and consistency; discretion should be structured; reasons for decisions should be given, and provision should be made for complaints and appeals. If there is already a degree of consensus about these principles underpinning civil liberties, political opposition to extending them into the field of welfare provision should not be formidable.

Developing procedural rights

In developing ideas on how to make procedural rights work in practice, we start with the assumption that it is possible and desirable for a society to share and express values and aspirations about what a welfare system should achieve. We then build on a set of judicial principles outlined by Galligan, and consider different areas of provision separately to see how these principles might usefully be applied. Each presents its own problems and possibilities. Certainly there are no universal solutions: procedures must be custom-made for the different services. This underscores our earlier point that the most productive way of introducing rights into welfare is likely to be piecemeal and experimental, but within the context of a shared set of values.

While it is not proposed that these new social rights be entrenched, an important question that remains is whether rights should be statutory or expressed in codes of practice or other non-statutory forms. Statutory rights can be enforced by individual citizens through the judicial process. The same is not normally true of rights expressed in codes of practice, although these can have considerable force, depending on their status. Some codes of practice are statutory (for example, schedules attached to Acts of Parliament); some are created by ministerial regulations; some are drawn up and administered by self-regulating bodies. Nick Doyle and Tessa Harding show in Chapter 4 how the Conservative Government retreated, in the 1990 NHS and Community Care Act, from the rights-based approach of the Disabled Persons Act 1986. The 1986 Act, if implemented, would have established a significant number of enforceable rights for disabled people. But the Conservatives in Government have since demonstrated a clear preference for conferring powers and duties on provider agencies.

In his chapter, Jonathan Montgomery looks in detail at aspects of health promotion and health care, and considers where it might be appropriate to introduce rights. He argues for a limited range of individually enforceable rights, to be enshrined in a new Rights of Patients Act: these would cover consent, confidentiality, access to records and the right to a second opinion. He proposes that they be enforceable in the first instance through a new complaints procedure, set up under the Act, with appeal to the courts. Legal assistance, but not legal aid, would be available to claimants. In addition, Montgomery argues for a Code of Patients' Rights provided for by the new Act. This would not have force of law but would set standards by which complaints would be assessed through the new complaints procedure, with appeal to the Health Service Commissioners.

Nina Biehal and others take a different approach in their chapter on social work. They examine in detail the problems posed at key stages of the relationship between social worker and service user: defining the problem to be dealt with; making choices and reaching agreements; and participating in decisions. They set out extensive proposals about how individual users (voluntary and involuntary clients') should expect to be treated, to be consistent with the principles of procedural fairness and the objectives of the service. They leave open the question of how these rights might be enforced. One suggestion is that procedural guidelines be issued, either through legislation or in the form of a Department of Health circular.

Both these chapters reveal a tension between the desire to confer genuine and empowering rights on individuals and the desire to avoid rigidity; to keep open the channels of democratic debate and to keep lawyers at bay. Dire warnings are regularly issued from across the Atlantic that if new rights are introduced in the UK, the lawyers will have a field day, huge sums of public (and private) money will be squandered, and to little effect except to enrich an already privileged profession. It has also been argued that in the US, where rights are plentiful and there are more lawyers per head of population than in any other country, litigation has become a substitute for political discourse. Contentious issues are sucked into the judicial process, where they are chewed over and swallowed up in interminable and unproductive lawsuits. And this, it is contended, makes it increasingly hard to mobilise democratic debate or action for political change.

There is both a pessimistic and an optimistic response to this cautionary tale. The first accepts that if it happens in the US it is bound to happen in the UK too, and concludes that we should retreat from the rights project and concentrate on strengthening our democratic processes. The second maintains that the UK can learn from the experience of others and develop routes for enforcing rights which do not inevitably fall into the same traps. For example, we can introduce new and improved complaints procedures; we can develop the role of the local Ombudsman, the Health Service Commissioners and (under a Labour Government) the revamped Audit or Quality Commission. We can resolve not to use courts where tribunals will do, and to strengthen advice and advocacy systems so that lawyers are brought in only as a last resort. All such possibilities should at least be investigated thoroughly before the pessimists are allowed to win the day. This work has yet to be done.

The idea that legally enforceable rights can weaken democracy is not a new one, but in the UK it has more often been put in terms of rights strengthening individuals and weakening collectives. If it is essential to a democracy that individuals should be able to join together and take concerted action in a common cause, but if relations between people and state are recognised only in terms of individual transactions between the lone citizen and the relevant state agency, what scope does that leave for the activities or legitimacy of groups and associations? Some individuals will be better able to enforce their rights than others; and in some circumstances the liberties and abilities of citizens are more effectively protected by groups than by individuals on their own. As Jonathan Montgomery suggests, and as IPPR has argued elsewhere, public policy should recognise the importance of group activity in the process of empowering individuals. Where appropriate, they should be encouraged to inform, advise, represent and act as advocates for their members. Most usefully, perhaps, groups could be supported with resources (space, shared expertise, equipment, etc.) The rights of appropriate associations to be consulted in policy formation, to participate in decisions and to pursue complaints and appeals could be promoted through legislation as well as through codes of practice. Here again, there is work yet to be done and, as suggested earlier, that work should address the problems of how far groups can be genuinely representative.

Wendy Thomson argues, from another standpoint, that some kinds of rights can weaken democracy by concentrating power in central government and the judiciary. Her account of developing local service agreements is based on practical experience in a local authority where residents negotiate through neighbourhood forums and user groups; the aims and priorities for local services, how they are to be delivered and what should happen if the agreement is breached. She contends that each agreement must be separately negotiated and customised to suit the needs expressed in particular neighbourhood and services. She warns that rights imposed from the centre could undermine the aims which they are intended to promote. The needs and preferences of different residents in different localities cannot be contained in uniform national standards and entitlements. If a service is to succeed in meeting diverse needs, people must be involved in determining what matters to them.

There are (at least) two possible rejoinders. The first is voiced by Thomson herself: the scope for service agreements of the kind she advocates is not infinite and, if overworked, could become counter-productive. To appreciate this point, one only has to imagine being invited by one's local council to attend meetings to negotiate separate agreements on every aspect of council provision (street lighting, roads, refuse collection, community care, education . . . the list is long). The second rejoinder is that the service-agreement approach is one in which the local authority initiates the action, determines its parameters and retains most of the power. Is there a case for individuals to have some rights which are independent of the council and which might be determined at a national level? It is too early to draw conclusions; the important thing, at this stage, is to have the debate. In the meantime it is worth pointing out that the principles of procedural fairness outlined by Galligan and developed by Doyle and Harding are often clearly reflected in the service agreements being negotiated at a local level. Thus, the two strategies suggested in these chapters – local agreements on the one hand and national rights, codes or guidelines on the other – have important areas of compatibility.

If citizens are to have rights or, indeed, to negotiate local agreements, who is to be involved and who, if anyone, should be excluded? Priscilla Alderson examines the case for children's rights, pointing out that children are excluded from important civil rights on grounds which have nothing to do with their competence as human beings. She argues that children should not be defined by age alone, but according to each individual's developing competence and the circumstances for which the decision is made. We do not deal here with the question of migrants deemed by law not to be citizens of the UK: this is another important area on which work has yet to be done.

It will be clear that we have not covered all the ground around the subject of welfare rights. Our aim has been to open a new debate by examining ideas about social rights and exploring ways of putting some of those ideas into practice. This is a highly complex field which offers no simple or immediate solutions: it requires a lot more investigation and a cautious, experimental approach. But we hope to have shown that the subject is worth pursuing.

Anna Coote

1992

1 CITIZENSHIP, RIGHTS AND WELFARE

Raymond Plant

During the past thirty to forty years those on the Left have become used to the idea of talking about welfare in terms of rights. The influence of T. H. Marshall was crucial: he argued in his great essay *Citizenship and Social Class* that the social and economic rights of citizenship provided the twentieth century's contribution to the idea of rights. Civil and political rights had been gradually won since the seventeenth century. However, it was in the modern period that rights came to be seen in terms of rights to resources (to welfare, health, education, income and social security) rather than being treated as immunities and being seen in terms of procedures such as due process of law or fair elections. This dimension of rights is also a central part of the United Nations Declaration of Human Rights: here, no sharp distinction is drawn between civil rights such as freedom from coercion and assault, political rights such as a right to vote and to political participation, and rights to health, education and welfare.

This is a fundamental shift in emphasis. Earlier it was assumed that civil and political rights alone were central to the status of citizenship. The level of economic well being people might be thought to enjoy, the education they could get and the degree to which they could enjoy health and health care were essentially private matters. They were private in the sense that they were to be attained through the market, by the individual's own efforts. Being a citizen did not imply a social and economic status so much as a political and civil one. Civil and political citizenship could be attained and enjoyed, so it was thought, despite the inequalities in social and economic status that would inevitably follow from this status being secured through the market. Of course, it was recognised that some would be unable to attain even a minimal status through the market. For the disabled and the feeble-minded the remedy was either private charity, or public provision under the Elizabethan Poor Law or, later, under the system introduced by the Poor Law Amendment Act 1834. But whether private or public, relief from poverty or from illness was not to be construed in terms of rights and citizenship. There could be no right to private charity since charity was essentially discretionary, a gift to which the recipient had no moral or legal right. In the case of public provision after 1834, there was certainly no right to resources. The indigent person's claim to relief was to be met only in a kind of contractual way: public provision was tied to a set of incentives to work and, for those within workhouses, to a punitive regime.

The idea that there is a right to welfare and to resources is a fundamental challenge to the idea that citizenship is only a civil and political status, and to the capitalist idea that a person's status in economic and social terms is to be determined by the market. The idea of rights to welfare has also become linked with the idea of social justice. According to this view, market outcomes should not be just accepted with all the resulting inequalities; rather, citizenship confers a right to a central set of resources which can provide economic security, health and education – and this right exists irrespective of a person's standing in the market.

The idea of welfare rights, contrary to some of the basic ideological assumptions of *laissez faire* capitalism, confers an economic and social status outside the market; it involves the idea of a just distribution of resources and, therefore, a correction of market outcomes. It also entails the idea that citizens' obligations do not stop at mutual non-interference, for citizens have positive obligations to provide resources for welfare which can be collected coercively through the tax system. Additionally, it implies some limit to commodification and commercialisation, in the sense that the basic welfare goods to which individuals have rights are not ultimately to be subject to the market mechanism, since the market cannot guarantee the provision of these goods, as of right, on a fair basis to all citizens. These social rights of citizenship are also to be ascribed independently of any character assessment of the individual bearer of social rights. They are unconditional, based upon the status of citizenship alone and not on whether the individual lives the kind of life that others in society would wish. In this respect, too, social rights are on a par with civil and political rights. Civil and political rights are not dependent on living a virtuous life; nor does one have to be a member of the deserving poor to qualify for social rights.

It is not surprising, therefore, that in the past fifteen years (which have seen the ideological ascendancy of capitalism and the intellectual retreat of socialism and social democracy) the idea of welfare rights should be high on the agenda for attack and criticism by the intellectual defenders of free markets. Part of this chapter will be concerned with looking at the nature of this attack and defending the intellectual and moral coherence of the view that welfare can be considered as a right.

However, I want first to explore another issue relating to social and economic rights. It might be thought that those who have followed Marshall, as well as Marshall himself, have made a kind of an intellectual error in thinking of these sorts of social and economic claims as rights in the first place. It might be argued that there is some kind of logical link between something being claimed as a right and the possibility of its enforceability. That is to say, what distinguishes a right from other things, such as desires or interests and claims, is that rights can be enforced. Critics then go on to argue that many social and economic rights are not enforceable, or they are non justiciable because in many cases, such as health and education, there is not and cannot be any mechanism for rendering such rights amenable to enforcement. I shall consider later why this might be thought to be so, but for the moment it looks like a powerful argument: rights must be connected to some mechanism of enforcement; there is no such mechanism for rights to health and education and hence they are not genuine rights. This is a particularly salient issue at the moment when there is a strong movement on the left towards constitutional reform and the entrench-ment of a Bill of Rights. Many on the Left have argued that such a Bill would be defective if it dealt only with civil and political rights. Others meanwhile argue that large parts of welfare cannot be considered in terms of rights in the necessarily strict sense of enforceability.

In this chapter then I shall try to do two things: first to demonstrate that social and economic rights are not in fact categorically different from civil and political rights as capitalist critics maintain; and second to consider ways in which such rights might in fact be enforced. This latter issue will connect with a currently salient political issue, namely the ideas about citizens' charters[1] being offered for consideration by all the main political parties. These can plausibly be regarded as attempts to identify ways in which individuals can come to have enforceable rights and entitlements to publicly provided goods. However, as currently presented, these various charters are not really put into a philosophical context which would provide them with a proper rationale. The argument of this chapter is that the idea of social and economic rights can provide such a rationale. Furthermore, it can link charters of social rights to a Bill of Rights to protect civil and political rights, so as to make them independent but parallel and mutually reinforcing ways of empowering citizens.

The critique of the social rights of citizenship

Before we can get to the practical political implications of this view, however, we need to grapple with some basic theoretical issues. While these may appear abstract, they do concern the underlying rationale of the idea that there can be genuine rights to social and economic resources and that citizenship has an intrinsic social and economic dimension as much as a civil and political one.

The New Right in its economic liberal form, as found for example in the writings of Hayek, Buchanan, Friedman, John Gray,[2] Norman Barry, Lord Joseph and others who contribute to the Institute of Economic Affairs and the Adam Smith Institute, has mounted a substantial onslaught on the idea of social and economic rights. That was to be expected: to accept such rights would pose a major threat to the coherence of free market capitalism.

The New Right argues, first of all, that such rights differ fundamentally from civil and political rights in terms of the corresponding duties which acceptance of these rights place upon citizens. It claims that the civil and political rights of citizenship imply corresponding duties of non-interference and abstaining from action. These rights are essentially about protecting a set of *negative* liberties or immunities, that is to say freedoms from interference of various sorts. The right to life is the right to be free from being killed, the right to freedom of speech is the right to speak and not to be silenced, the rights to physical integrity and security are rights to be free from assault, rape and coercion of various sorts. Because these are rights to be free from interference of specific types, the corresponding duties on the part of fellow citizens, government and social agencies are to abstain from killing, interfering, raping, coercing and so forth. The right to life is not the positive right to the means to life. This is a distinction of the first importance for understanding the critique of *positive* rights to resources put forward by the New Right.

First of all, it is assumed that because civil and political rights are rights not to be interefered with in specific ways, they are always capable of being respected since the corresponding duties are essentially duties to abstain from action; duties of abstinence are in fact costless and can therefore always be discharged. Social and economic rights however, are categorically different in the sense that they always imply the commitment of resources and in that sense are always going to involve costs. If the resources are not in fact available then the rights cannot be met. Social rights always run up against resource constraints and therefore there is always a possibility of their not being respected – unlike negative rights, which imply costless duties and therefore can always be respected.

Second, because social and economic rights run up against resource constraints these resources may have to be rationed, which undermines the idea that they can in fact be rights. If something is a right then it ought to be able to be claimed in an unconditional way. This cannot be true of social rights. From this it follows that social rights are inherently non justiciable in that there cannot be a legally enforceable right to a scarce resource.

It is also argued that the defender of social rights operates with a defective view of liberty. Civil and political rights essentially codify a set of negative liberties; social rights, however, seem to trade on an idea of positive freedom – to be able to do certain things for which health, education and income are necessary. Social rights therefore seem to link the idea of freedom and ability, implying that being free to do something is the same as being able to do it and therefore having the appropriate resources to do it. If we have a right to liberty then we have a right to those resources which bear directly upon our capacity for agency and our ability to act freely.

In the view of the neo-liberal critics of social rights this is a fundamentally mistaken notion of freedom. Freedom has to be distinguished sharply from ability. No-one is able to do all that they are free to do. To assimilate the two, so that freedom implies ability and thus a right to those resources which would enable one to what one is free to do, is just conceptual confusion. Freedom has to be restricted to negative liberty in terms of *freedom from*, and the rights that protect those liberties are essentially negative rights.

It is also argued that underlying the idea of positive rights is a concept of needs: that people have a need for certain sorts of resources in order to live adequately. However, it is then argued that the idea of needs is essentially open-ended and therefore that the needs which underpin positive rights are also open-ended – and thus social rights themselves are without any clear limit. They can and will expand inexorably under interest group pressure, since there is no clear limit to health, welfare and education. It is claimed that the position is fundamentally different with civil and political rights. Here, there are clear limits to the rights and, since the duties connected with them are ones of abstinence, these duties are clear, categorical, always capable of being discharged; they will not grow inexorably. We know when we have discharged our negative duty not to interfere with someone under the negative right to security. We do not have such a clear idea of what our duty is with regard to a positive right to security – in terms of the resources necessary to provide it – since the content of that right can expand.

The link between the ideas of social rights and social justice is also rejected by critics. What fuels the argument for social rights is the concern with the alleged unjust outcome of pure market allocations. Because markets cause injustice for the worst off there is then a claim that there should be a collective responsibility to correct market outcomes in terms of justice, by conferring on all citizens a right to those resources which may not be secured to each person in a fair and predictable manner by the market. This claim is disputed by the New Right for several reasons.

It is argued first of all that the idea of social justice is incurably vague and contested. In a morally pluralist society it is not possible to arrive at a consensus about social justice. We can distribute resources according to a wide range of criteria: merit, need, desert, entitlement, equality, and so forth. There is no uniquely compelling criterion or principle on which citizens in a pluralistic society can actually agree and thus the idea that social justice can ground a set of welfare rights is a delusion.

In addition it is claimed that markets do not produce injustice in terms of their outcomes. If people experience poverty or disadvantage in markets, then so long as these outcomes are the consequence of individual acts of free exchange, then no injustice is caused. The argument here trades on the idea that injustice has to be caused by intentional action. However, the distribution of income and wealth produced by markets is not intended by anyone and therefore injustice cannot arise. Market distributions arise as the result of millions of individual acts of free exchange. This cannot produce injustice because market outcomes are unintended. Hence there is no moral case for a set of citizen rights to resources, conferred outside the market by political means, being based on an idea of social justice, because that idea is illusory.

It is further claimed that if social justice were supposed to govern the distribution of resources, public authorities charged with distributing those resources would have to act in arbitrary and discretionary ways. The argument is that we lack a clear idea about the appropriate principles of just distribution, whether based on need, desert, equality or any other criterion; we cannot therefore write rules of law which could govern just distribution. This is part of Hayek's critique in the second volume of Law, *Legislation and Liberty*: a regime of social justice would strengthen the hands of professionals and bureaucrats in the public sector who are charged with the task of operating justly in a context in which there cannot be any clear rules of justice since we lack the social consensus that would underpin these rules. This would entrench at the heart of the public sector a wholly undesirable, but equally unavoidable degree of professional and bureaucratic power since such resources under their control would have to be distributed and rationed in an ethical vacuum in which there cannot be any rules of justice to guide the rationing of scarce resources.

A defence of social rights

The arguments outlined above add up to a pretty fundamental assault on the idea of social rights and there are clear practical implications for the public sector. Essentially it puts the whole weight of citizenship on the civil and political realms. The public sector is not to be construed as essential to citizenship. Few of the New Right are now arguing for wholesale privatisation of the public sector, but this has more to do with political possibility than with any belief in the principle that citizenship entails a right to public provision of resources and services. It has to be remembered that in 1983 a paper sponsored by Sir Geoffery Howe and prepared by the Central Policy Review Staff did in fact argue for a thorough privatisation of state-provided services. What defeated the proposal was the ensuing outcry and the need to win the 1983 election, not the thought that it might be inappropriate to privatise services which were to be seen as a right of citizenship. Obviously, if one does see provision of social resources in terms of rights then there is an objection of principle to their wholesale privatisation, because no market can possibly guarantee delivering these basic resources as rights of citizenship.

Implicit in this argument are two profoundly different philosophies of the public sector and public provision. There are also two contrasting views of the nature of citizenship. One sees it in civil and political terms. The other sees it not only in those terms but also in social and economic terms, and contends that the freedoms and immunities which are guaranteed in a Bill of civil and political rights remain wholly abstract if people do not have the social and economic resources to be independent citizens.

So can the critique of social rights in fact be met? In my view most of the arguments outlined above are extremely weak. They are weak either in an absolute sense, in that they are not very good arguments, or because, if they were to be accepted, then they would apply equally to civil and political rights. Those who criticise social rights are not usually impugning civil and political rights as well, yet if they take their own strictures on social rights seriously this might well be the consequence of their own arguments.

The first argument against social rights trades on the idea of scarcity. Social rights intrinsically involve the commitment of scarce resources and there cannot be a right to scarce resources. However, it is difficult to see why this argument does not apply equally to civil and political rights. While these rights are essentially rights to be left alone in various ways, with corresponding duties of abstinence, nevertheless in the real world those rights have to be enforced and methods of enforcement involve the costs of police, courts, prisons, etc. It might be argued that this is a more incidental feature of civil and political rights, whereas costs are intrinsic to social rights. However, this is doubtful. What is it that marks something out as a right? If it is that rights, unlike other claims, have to be *enforceable* then there has to be an enforcement mechanism and therefore, the costs of enforceability are intrinsic to all sorts of rights, not just social ones. To put the point more simply, if one believes that there is a right to the protection and enforceability of rights (and how would they be rights otherwise?) then one cannot draw a sharp distinction between one set of rights and another by arguing that one set intrinsically involves costs and thus the commitment of scarce resources, while the other does not. If we have a right to enforceable civil and political rights then this is a positive right to resources.

It is argued by critics that there cannot be a right to, for example, the services of a doctor or teacher, since these are inherently in short supply, compared with the potential need. Again, though, it is difficult to see that this marks out social rights as uniquely problematic. There must be a right to the protection of civil and political rights, but there cannot be a right to the services of a policeman, as these are subject to the same problems of scarcity as doctors and teachers. It is currently illegal for a chief constable, as a matter of policy, not to enforce a particular set of laws. Nevertheless a chief constable has to decide how to deploy his forces and individual members of the public have no legally enforceable right to particular policing services in relation to any specific incident, any more than they have rights to the services of a doctor or teacher. It is difficult therefore to believe that the difference between civil and political rights on the one hand and social rights on the other, can be defined in terms of costs – once it is accepted that there is, in effect, a *positive right to the protection of negative rights.*

The same argument applies to the duties that go with rights. The critic of social rights argues that the duties that correspond to negative rights are clear and categorical and involve abstaining from action and interference; whereas the duties corresponding to social rights always involve resources and are therefore inherently vague and open ended. You never know, according to this critique, when enough has been done to satisfy the claims embodied in social rights. Such rights and the corresponding duties are always going to be subject to political possibility and political negotiation, but this is not true of civil and political rights. However, if the argument outlined above goes through, then again the distinction cannot be upheld. Let us take two examples: the right to privacy and the right to physical security. In the case of the latter, as we have seen, the enforceability of that right depends on the police force and the degree of enforceability depends on the resources available to the police. The amount of resources which we as a society decide to allocate to the police to defend these sorts of rights is as much a matter of political negotiation as are the resources allocated to health care or education. In the case of the right to privacy it can be argued that the resources needed to enforce this right also change with time. The invention of information technology has created new possibilities for infringing this right and new mechanisms are needed to protect and enforce it. Again, the resources we commit to this are going to vary and will depend upon political negotiation and political judgement. It is not the case, therefore, that civil and political rights are in some way pure and unsullied and detached from the sordid world of political decision-making. Both sorts of rights, as enforceable claims, necessarily involve resources – and the quality and quantity of resources will depend on politics.

This brings us to needs. The critics' argument here is that an idea of needs underpins the claim to social resources embodied in the doctrine of social rights. However, say the critics, the idea of needs is vague and open ended and therefore social rights can expand without clear limit, turning more and more of civil society away from private provision for which the individual is responsible towards politically conferred rights. Again, the assumption is that civil and political rights are clear and obvious and do not have this tendency to expand. It is also argued that in relation to health and, to some degree, education too, there is an interaction between needs and technological change, because needs develop with advances in technology. The discovery of ways of treating heart disease with bypass surgery has created a whole class of new needs; the invention of the computer has created a whole class of educational needs. This again leads to the expansion of social rights and with it public expenditure and the growth of the public sector.

Yet here, too, it is difficult to draw sharp distinctions between civil and political rights and social rights. Presumably such rights as freedom from assault or interference, or rights to privacy and physical integrity, are rooted in some idea of what the basic needs and interests of citizens are. These needs too may be without clearly defined limits. Physical security depends on all sorts of things from police forces to street lighting and there is always more that could be done. Also these needs change with technology. As we have already seen the need for privacy changes in relation to information technology; the need for physical security, for example, in air travel has changed since the invention of plastic explosives and depends upon newly invented security devices. Again the enforceability of rights in relation to such needs changes with technology and it is not possible to draw a categorical distinction between two sorts of rights on these terms.

It is also difficult to see that questions of social justice can be avoided in relation to the enforceability of civil and political rights. Once it is accepted that the enforceability of these rights involves costs and resources and thus political negotiation and political decision, then there are going to be questions about the fair distribution of resources *between* different types of public expenditure to meet different sorts of rights; about the fair distribution *within* particular sorts of rights (such as physical security or privacy to take the two examples discussed earlier); and about the fair distribution of resources *between* particular sections of the population in regard to such rights. If, as New Right critics argue, we do not have a sense of social justice as a society, then it is difficult to see that this claim does not impinge directly on the distribution of resources to protect civil and political rights, just as it does with social rights.

The critics argue that we do not have such a conception in a pluralistic society. However, the issues with which we are concerned here have to do with needs of various sorts, whether these needs be to do with a sense of autonomy and therefore being free from interference, a sense of physical integrity and a sense of private space, or with security of income, or with education or health. It would be a very ardent relativist who could deny that there is a consensus that income, health, education and welfare are needs bearing on the capacity for agency,[3] which all citizens in have in common in a society like ours.

Of course, there might be an argument that even if we accept that these are common needs, there is in fact no consensus about how to satisfy them in relation to social rights. This argument has to be treated with some care. Up to a point it might be true – in the sense that there may be no consensus on where the limits of public provision should be set. However two comments are apposite at this point. The first is that yet again there is no reason to think that this is uniquely a problem for social rights. Take again the right to physical security and the right to privacy: the limits of provision to meet these rights might well be controversial and a matter of political dispute.

Second, we are able through political negotiation to get some degree of consensus, despite these differences, on what it is fair to allocate to help to enforce these rights and there is no reason of principle why this should not equally be so in regard to the resources allocated to meet social rights. Obviously this consensus can only be built politically if there is an agreement that there has to be some limit at any particular time on the resources to meet these sorts of needs. But there does not seem to be any reason of principle why it should not be possible to develop a consensus about what it is reasonable to do and then to define rights in relation to this consensus. This idea will be explored more fully later. The main point for the moment though is that if all rights involve the commitment of resources then the issue of social justice in their distribution will arise for all of them – since the very fact that they are rights means that the resources involved in their protection cannot be left wholly to markets. Once there is public provision to protect rights then questions about the fair allocation of resources are bound to arise. If the New Right's critique of social justice is allowed to stand in the sense that we accept that we cannot develop through political negotiation a conception of a fair allocation of resources, then the problems here will arise in relation not only to social rights, but to other rights as well.

The critic's view of the moral redundancy of social justice does not, in any case, hold water. They argue that free markets cannot produce injustice in distribution since the outcomes of markets are not intentional and the question of injustice can only arise when it has been caused by intentional action. This argument is defective because our moral responsibility for the consequences of our actions arises not just in relation to the *intended* consequences but also the *foreseeable* consequences. If it is a foreseeable consequence of extending markets, let us say in the field of health care or education, that the worst off may actually not experience as much welfare as they would under public provision, then while this may not be anyone's intention, if it is a foreseeable consequence then there is a case for saying that we bear moral responsibility for those consequences, even though they are not intended. If the general principle here is accepted, namely that we are responsible for the foreseeable albeit unintended consequences of our actions, then the issue becomes an empirical one: the extent to which consequences are foreseeable and what in fact they are in relation to the worst-off groups in society. If this is accepted, then there is scope for a moral critique of markets in terms of social justice and for conferring on citizens rights to resources as a matter of social justice, given that they would not be able to command those resources in the market and this failure is socially unjust. Hence, there is moral purchase in the idea of social justice and an idea of social justice can in fact underpin a set of welfare rights.

The critics will still argue that social rights are defective because they trade upon a false conception of liberty. Liberty has to be defined in terms of the absence of intentional coercion and these liberties are secured by civil and political rights which define the limits of legitimate and illegitimate coercion. Social rights, according to this view, operate with a false view of liberty, namely that liberty is linked with ability and the associated resources that people need to exercise liberty. This argument is central to the Hayek-inspired critique of social rights and the roots of the argument are to be found in *The Constitution of Liberty*. However, while the issue is extremely complex there are at least three arguments that reduce the force of this centrally important critique. The first is that if liberty is categorically different from ability, then we seem to be involved in a paradox. If there is no possibility of performing an action, that is, we are clearly unable to do it (like jumping from Southampton to New York), then the question of whether we are free to do it does not arise. If this is accepted then it cannot be true that liberty and ability are categorically different. Rather the possibility of doing x is a necessary condition of whether we are free or unfree to do x.

Second, if liberty is defined in terms of the absence of intentional coercion, then the issue of whether society A is more free than society B is to be settled by identifying and counting the range of intentionally coercive actions permitted in each society. This might make a very primitive society with few regulations and forms of interference more free than modern western society. Few would be prepared to accept this and the reason for not accepting it would be that in our sort of society we are in fact able to do far more things. If this is the reason for regarding our society as more free than a primitive society then again freedom and ability cannot be regarded as categorically different. The judgement turns on an evaluation of what people are able to do in these societies, and the normative judgement that some of the things they are *able* to do in one are more important than those they are able to do in another.

Third, there is the question of the worth of negative liberty. Why do we want to be free from coercion? Presumably we find liberty in the sense of being free from coercion valuable because of the range of things that we are able to do within the space secured by mutual non-coercion. If this is so then freedom and ability are not categorically different since what makes freedom valuable to us is what we are able to do with it. If this is rejected by New Right critics, then they have to explain why human beings value freedom and, if they are to be consistent in separating freedom from ability, this answer has to make no reference to ability and what people are enabled to do. There is no compelling reason for rejecting the idea of social rights on the ground that it trades on a false view of freedom: it does not.

Finally, the critic argues, as we have seen, that because social rights are rights to scarce resources there has to be rationing and this in turn means that public officials will have to act in arbitrary and discretionary ways in the distribution of resources and this in turn will entrench professional power which cannot be made accountable. This is certainly a problem, and will be the focus of the rest of the chapter. However, again the problem is exactly the same in relation to civil and political rights. In the same way as the hospital consultant has the professional discretion to ration scarce resources, so the chief constable has to choose how to allocate resources to protect civil and political rights.

It is therefore false to think that there is an account of civil and political rights that is pristine and pure and does not involve all the problems that critics ascribe to social rights. Both sets of rights involve much the same sorts of difficulty and it would be better to think through these common difficulties, rather than falsely assuming that all the problems can be laid at the door of social rights.

Rights, scarcity and discretion

The central practical issue is how to define a set of rights, against a background of scarcity, in terms of those things which are necessary to enforce them and make them a reality – whether these be hospital services, educational institutions or the police. Is there really any way to secure the enforceability of social rights at the individual level? This has not been properly confronted in the literature since Marshall put social rights of citizenship on to the political agenda in *Citizenship and Social Class*. The assumption has been that the general provision of public services is what social rights require, but equally it is clear that these have not led, by and large, to individually enforceable rights. If the idea of rights is linked to the idea of enforceability, then Marshallian social rights are actually a bit of a sham, and in fact possibly a rather cruel deception. People might think that they do have individually enforceable rights when they do not. The Secretary of State for Health has a general duty to maintain a national health service, but this does not yield an enforceable right to health care of a specific sort to individuals. The central issue then becomes whether this can be remedied at all, and, if not, whether it is sensible to carry on speaking the language of rights.

The point also links to professional power and discretion. If individuals do not have enforceable rights and the distribution of services is to a large degree at the discretion of professional providers, then the providers of services have every incentive to provide them on terms that suit them – rather than seeing themselves as responding to the rights of individuals to a set of services or resources. The idea of rights therefore can be seen as a way of empowering the citizen in the public sector in relation to those services which are provided, in response to the idea that there is a social dimension to citizenship. This idea of linking rights and entitlements to empowerment is a new one and marks a departure from the traditional approaches of both Right and Left.

On the Right it has been assumed too frequently that the only way to empower the individual is as a consumer in the marketplace and therefore that the only real way of empowering people in the public sector is by transferring publicly provided resources to the market. However, leaving aside the question of whether market empowerment is as powerful as people believe, there are crucial problems in privatising public services such as health and education. Of course, this is not a real political possibility at present, but I have tried, earlier in this chapter, to give reasons why we should not go down that road in any case. These services should be seen as an integral part of citizenship, supporting its political and civil aspects. Those from the Right who are now pressing the case for a citizen's charter seem to see it as a second best to privatisation and a way of strengthening market mechanisms within the public sector, which on their view is the only effective way of empowering people.

On the Left the issue of professional power in the public sector has often been seen in terms of greater regulation or democratisation. The only way to limit professional power is either to make it accountable to a higher bureaucratic level such as an inspectorate or a regulatory body, or to make professional power more accountable to democratic bodies. There are considerable problems with both of these approaches. In the case of bureaucratic regulation, it is difficult to believe that this empowers the citizen in any direct or meaningful way and there is also the problem that the inspectors or the regulators, in order to know what they are doing, have to come from the same professional groups as those whom they are regulating and are therefore in danger of 'going native' and being persuaded more by the needs of the professionals than by the rights of the citizen.

The case with democratic accountability is rather different, but it is quite difficult to have confidence in the view that elected representatives can in fact effectively monitor and hold to account the behaviour of professionals. First, there is an asymmetry of information in the sense that the professional has much more knowledge and experience of what he or she is doing than an amateur representative. This may well inhibit effective control and accountability in the delivery of services. Second, there is an asymmetry of motivation in that the professional provider of services has a greater incentive to limit the degree to which his or her activity is monitored than the elected representative has to get to the bottom of what is going on. We do not have to look very far to see ways in which professional service providers have frequently been able to get away with quite outrageous practices while elected representatives were wholly ignorant not just of particular practices in individual cases but rather a whole policy. The recent 'pin-down' case is the most blatant example of an elected social services committee not having any idea of a practice over a number of years in the residential homes run by professionals who were nominally accountable to elected representatives.

The idea of rights in the public sector provides a new way forward between the market and democracy as two models of empowerment. This is not to decry either markets or democracy, only to say that there is a case for looking at a new way and seeing how far we can get with it. If these rights can work and be made clear and enforceable, whether they are rights to have certain procedures followed, or actual rights to resources, then this would clearly be a more direct way of empowering the citizen than either the market, or bureaucratic regulation, or greater democratic accountability. Rights will not be a panacea and there will be areas of the public sector where we shall have to rely on both inspection and greater democratic accountability, but rights should be looked at very carefully on a case-bycase basis to see how far they can be taken.

It is essential, if they are to be more than rhetorical, that these rights be linked to enforcement procedures, and to compensation or the provision of alternatives if the rights fail. There will be different mechanisms in different areas. For example, there can be changes to the contracts of public service professionals, as doctors' and teachers' contracts have already been changed, specifying more clearly what their duties are. There can be administrative definitions of rights, particularly in relation to procedures. There can be a requirement to meet performance indicators with the possibility, if these are not met, of individuals being able to go elsewhere for a service, or receive compensation – and so forth. In certain circumstances, vouchers might be a way of empowering individuals with an individually enforceable right. Indeed, contrary to the typical New Right view, which wants to deny social rights altogether, vouchers are a defensible mechanism for securing welfare rights. The case for using them has to be discussed in empirical terms rather than ideological ones, whether on the Right or on the Left. If there are genuine rights to welfare, as this chapter has argued, then vouchers should be carefully considered as one of a number of mechanisms for securing such individually enforceable rights.

Different mechanisms are considered in the chapters that follow. Where they can be made to work, these changes will strengthen the social dimensions of citizenship, as well as helping to strengthen civil and political rights and increasing the accountability of service providers to the citizens whose needs and interests they are supposed to serve.

Hence, it is important to put the idea of citizens' charters in the context of a new philosophy of the public sector. Public provision should not be seen as second best to the market as it is by the New Right. Nor should be it be dominated by service providers, as a consequence of the idealistic but rather limited assumption on the Left that democratisation can increase the power of the ordinary citizen in relation to professionally organised bureaucracies. Instead, we have an opportunity to embrace a new philosophy of the public sector, based upon the social rights of citizenship – one which is not only consistent with civil and political rights, but would also enhance the quality of citizenship in those spheres.

2 A SOCIAL CHARTER FOR BRITAIN

Norman Lewis and Mary Seneviratne

The classic civil and political rights, such as the right to life and freedom of expression, are commonly seen as fit subjects for a constitutional Bill of Rights. We argue in this chapter that people also have basic rights to well being and to share in the nation's prosperity – and that these should be enshrined in a 'Social Charter' as part of British law. It is not a new concept: indeed, the UK is already a party to international treaties and conventions which seek to guarantee these rights. What we shall argue is that these international obligations should be brought on to the domestic agenda.

In support of our case, we have drawn up a draft charter. It is purely illustrative. Others will identify omissions and, no doubt, some of our inclusions will be controversial. Our draft is an attempt to engender debate.

The European Social Charter

The most important international agreement on social rights to which the UK is a party is the European Social Charter (ESC) of the Council of Europe, which was adopted in 1961 and came into force in 1965. We shall discuss other international and European obligations later, but we shall first consider the ESC, since it provides in our view the most useful basis for a charter of social rights within the UK.

The Council of Europe was founded in 1949 to foster greater unity and co-operation between the people and nations of Europe. It is now one of the largest of the European political institutions, and its aims include the improvement of living conditions, the development of human values, and the upholding of principles of parliamentary democracy and human rights.

The Council is best known for its work on human rights and, indeed, a fundamental aspect of membership is that states must recognise the principle of the rule of law, and guarantee their citizens human rights and fundamental freedoms. The European Convention on Human Rights was drawn up and signed in 1950, and came into force in 1953. Less well known is the European Social Charter (ESC), yet the Council of Europe maintains that these two agreements should be taken together as the buttress upholding the fundamental rights of the individual. While the European Convention on Human Rights is principally aimed at protecting civil and political rights, the ESC seeks to protect rights in the social and economic sphere.

The preamble of the ESC defines its aims: to secure the enjoyment of social rights without discrimination, to improve standards of living, and to promote the social well being of the populations of those states which are parties to the Charter. The ESC is interpreted in the light of this preamble.

Part I of the ESC lists nineteen rights which are dealt with in more detail in Part II. Articles 1 to 8 are concerned with rights relating to employment, or what might be termed 'economic' rights. The other 'social' rights include:

* the right to protection of health (Article 11);
* the right to social security (Article 12);
* the right to social and medical assistance (Article 13);
* the right to benefit from social welfare services (Article 14);
* the right of the family to social, legal and economic protection (Article 16);
* the right of mothers and children to social and economic protection (Article 17).

Rights relating to vocational training are dealt with in Articles 9, 10 and 15. These concern:

* the right to vocational guidance;
* the right to vocational training;
* the right of the physically or mentally disabled to vocational training, rehabilitation and social resettlement.

Foreign workers are protected by Articles 18 and 19, which provide:

* a right to engage in gainful occupation in the territory of other contracting parties;
* rights for migrant workers and their families to protection and assistance.

The obligations contained in these nineteen Articles are set out in detail, in a series of numbered paragraphs, each requiring a separate undertaking by the contracting states.

A Protocol to the ESC, adopted in 1988, is not yet in force. It adds four more rights:

* the right to equal opportunities and equal treatment in matters of employment and occupation without discrimination on the grounds of sex (Article 1);
* the right to information and consultation at the workplace (Article 2);
* the right to take part in the determination and improvement of

working conditions and the working environment (Article 3);

* the right of elderly persons to social protection, the provision of adequate resources, of housing adapted to their needs, and rights for those in institutional care (Article 4).

Under Part III of the Charter, the contracting parties undertake to consider Part I of the Charter 'as a declaration of the aims which it will pursue by all appropriate means'. Parties must also be bound by at least five of what are considered to be key undertakings,[1] and by at least 10 of the 19 Articles in their entirety, or 45 of the 72 numbered paragraphs which make up the Articles.

The UK has agreed to be bound by all except seven[2] of the paragraphs relating to rights in the workplace. So far as 'social' rights are concerned, the UK has undertaken to establish or maintain a system of social security.[3] It has not, however, agreed to be bound by three paragraphs which would oblige it to maintain social security at certain minimum standards, to endeavour to raise it progressively to a higher level, and to ensure equal treatment for nationals of other contracting parties in relation to social security.[4]

In the UK, international treaties do not have the force of law. Ratification of a treaty is an executive act, and legislation is required to incorporate it into domestic law. There has been no such Act of Parliament in relation to the European Social Charter. Such force as it has in relation to the practice of British governments therefore depends either on individual statutory enactments, or on the effectiveness of its enforcement procedures.

While the European Convention on Human Rights was agreed upon relatively quickly (it took one year to negotiate), the ESC proved more problematic. There were wide differences in the economic and social circumstances of the member states of the Council of Europe. Moreover, the nature of these rights – which are difficult to quantify precisely, may demand positive action and often require a commitment of resources – made it hard for member states to reach agreement. It is for these reasons that a particular method of enforcement has been adopted for the ESC which is different from that adopted for the Convention, and less demanding.

Part IV of the Charter deals with enforcement or, more accurately, with supervising its application. The contracting parties undertake to report every two years to the Secretary General of the Council of Europe on measures taken to apply such provisions of the Charter as they have accepted.[5] These reports are drawn up according to a *pro forma*, which contains detailed questions designed to elicit information showing how far the parties are abiding by their obligations. The reports are scrutinised by a Committee of Independent Experts, drawn from all the member states of the Council of Europe. There are currently seven such experts.

After studying the biennial reports, the Committee forms 'conclusions' on the extent to which the provisions of the Charter have been applied. The conclusions and the national reports are then sent to the Governmental Committee on the European Social Charter. This Committee consists of representatives of the contracting states, and it presents a report to the Parliamentary Assembly. Following a report by its Social and Health Affairs Committee, the Parliamentary Assembly submits an opinion to the Committee of Ministers. The Committee of Ministers, after examining all the various documents, is called upon to 'make to each contracting party any necessary recommendations'.[6] (The problems and criticisms of the ESC's method of enforcement will be dealt with in more detail later, p.40.)

Other relevant treaties

Another instrument of the Council of Europe is the European Code of Social Security and Protocol, which was adopted in 1964 and came into force in 1968. This also deals with matters relevant to a British Social Charter. The UK has signed and ratified five types of provision under the Code. These concern medical care, sickness benefit, unemployment benefit, old-age benefit, and family benefit.[7] The UK is not a party to those sections relating to employment injury benefit, invalidity benefit and survivors' benefit.[8] Nor has it ratified the Protocol. Enforcement of the Code is similar to that of the ESC, with contracting parties submitting annual reports to the Secretary-General of the Council of Europe.

In 1972, the Council of Europe adopted the European Convention on Social Security (and a Supplementary Agreement for its application). It came into force in 1977, but has not been ratified by the UK.

The Council of Europe's First Protocol to the Convention for the Protection of Human Rights and Fundamental Freedoms states that no person 'shall be denied the right to education'. This is a negative, rather than a positive duty: education is omitted altogether from the ESC. In our view a charter of social rights could contain positive rights in relation to education, particularly as education is the key to employment opportunities, and to vocational training. However, its inclusion in a British Social Charter would depend on whether such a charter were part of a larger human rights package (see below, p.37).

In addition to its obligations as a member of the Council of Europe, the UK is bound by the laws of the European Community (EC). Here, work is in progress to institute a Community Charter of Fundamental Social Rights. Would this make a better model for a British Social Charter? It will certainly be useful to have such a charter within the EC, but there are good reasons for keeping the ESC as our model. First, the EC itself has acknowledged the value of using the precedents set by the ESC; its declared intention is not to devise a new instrument, but to enshrine in Community law fundamental social guarantees which already exist in international conventions.

Second, while the EC Social Charter has yet to be agreed upon, the ESC is well established and has a long history; the UK has already accepted many of the obligations it entails. We can study the record of the ESC and examine the problems, particularly in relation to enforcement; lessons learned from this experience will be useful in developing proposals for a domestic charter.

Third, the European Community's concerns have until recently focused on developing a common market. There is now pressure to adopt a broader perspective, and to provide a charter to deal with such issues as labour policy, social security, health and environment. The outcome may resemble the ESC, but it starts from a different premise. The EC remains primarily concerned with economic rights; the aim of its Social Charter is expressed in terms of improving the social life and standards of living of workers and their families.

By contrast, the impetus for the ESC came not from a common economic policy, but from a shared belief in human rights and social justice. It was drawn up to deal with the social and economic aspects of the UN Declaration of Human Rights, just as the European Convention on Human Rights was designed to deal with its civil and political aspects. A recent decision to transfer responsibility for the ESC from the Social and Economic Affairs Directorate to the Human Rights Directorate of the Council of Europe re-affirms the link between them, and enhances the moral authority of the ESC. This is important in our view, because entitlement should be based on citizenship and on the person as a social being, rather than on the person as an economic being.

The United Nations Universal Declaration of Human Rights was adopted and proclaimed by the UN General Assembly in 1948. The purpose of this Declaration was principally to guarantee political and civil rights, but it also seeks to guarantee rights that can be classified as social or economic:

* the right to marry and found a family, and the right of the family to be protected by society and the state (Article 16);

* the right to social security (Article 22);

* the right to a standard of living adequate for health and well-being, which includes food, clothing, housing and medical care and necessary social services, and the right to security in the event of unemployment, sickness, disability, widowhood, old-age or other lack of livelihood in circumstances beyond the individual's control (Article 25);

* motherhood and childhood are entitled to special care and assistance, and all children, whether born in or out of wedlock, are entitled to the same social protection (Article 25);

* education is to be free at least in the elementary and fundamental stages, and to be compulsory in the elementary stage; technical and

professional education should be made generally available, and higher
education should be equally accessible to all on the basis of merit
(Article 26).

The UN Declaration was not intended to impose legal obligations on states, but
rather as a statement of principles which all states should observe, and of goals
for states to pursue. It was adopted unanimously. The UN then began work on
the two related areas of human rights: civil and political rights, and social and
economic rights. This resulted in two separate Covenants. The International
Covenant on Civil and Political Rights (1966) has little general relevance to
social and welfare rights, although it does speak about the protection of the
family (Article 23), which would be endorsed in the Charter proposed here. The
second Covenant is of more direct interest.

The International Covenant on Economic, Social and Cultural Rights
(1966) is based on the premise that the ideal of free human beings enjoying
freedom from fear and want can only be achieved if conditions are created
whereby 'everyone may enjoy his economic, social and cultural rights, as well as
his civil and political rights' (preamble). It calls upon states:

* to give protection and assistance to the family, including special
  protection for mothers before and after childbirth, with associated leave
  from work with pay or social-security benefits (Article 10);
* to recognise rights to adequate standards of living, including adequate
  food, clothing and housing and the continuous improvement in living
  conditions (Article 11);
* to create conditions to ensure that all people have the right to
  medical services in the event of sickness, in recognition of the right to
  enjoy high standards of physical and mental health (Article 12);
* to provide free, compulsory primary education for all, and actively to
  pursue the development of a system of schools at all levels (Article 13).

Both the UN Covenants have been signed and ratified by the UK, and both are
implemented by a supervisory system, based on periodic reports detailing the
measures adopted and the progress made in relation to these rights. There is also
an Optional Protocol to the Covenant on Civil and Political Rights, which gives
a right to individual petition. Thirty-eight states have signed and ratified this,
but the UK is not among them. Under the Covenant on Economic, Social and
Cultural Rights, reports are submitted to the Secretary-General of the United
Nations, who submits copies to the Economic and Social Council (Article 16).
As in the case of the ESC, this reporting system is open to criticism, as it depends
upon governments cooperating in providing full information. As we argue
below, p.47, there is a case for involving non-governmental organisations and
pressure groups in a reporting procedure of this kind.

To a large extent, a British Social Charter would reflect obligations already accepted by the UK in the international sphere; these represent a political commitment which can be built upon. The next step is to translate these international obligations into domestic policy.

Content and status of a British Social Charter

It is argued in the previous chapter that civil and political rights are inseparable from social and economic rights, and that there is no plausible case for affording the latter inferior status. IPPR has elsewhere proposed a Bill of Rights as part of a written constitution, and it has called for a reformed judiciary to enforce these rights.[9] We take the view that the package will not be complete without a Social Charter. In this section, we set out our proposals for the content and status of that Charter.

For the most part, we urge the adoption of the main Articles of the ESC, though with some important amendments and additions. First, we have excluded most of the workplace rights: we have done this because labour law and codes are relatively discrete, and because they impinge on many other international codes and conventions which complicate the picture considerably. Moreover, we assume that the EC, through some version of its Social Charter, will take the lead in this field. (The Community Charter of Fundamental Social Rights contains twelve Articles or rights; its inspiration has been the International Labour Organisation and the ESC. The Articles include the right to social protection and rights for the elderly and disabled, but its concentration is primarily on the workplace.) Some tangential workplace issues – training, for example – are included in our proposals, where they seem to us to have direct bearing on the generic good of social and economic well-being. We recognise that the division between the two sets of rights is by no means clear-cut. For example, it is becoming widely accepted that steps to remove discrimination in employment are no longer concerned solely with access to employment and working conditions, but should be part of an overall policy designed to ensure social and legal equality between different sections of society.

Second, we go beyond the ESC obligations where they seem to us to be pusillanimous; we also indicate where we think a British Social Charter should accede to ideas expressed in the ESC even where they have not been formally ratified by the UK.

We have excluded education on the ground that the right to education is traditionally included in a package of civil and political rights (as in the European Convention). Our proposals are based on the assumption that if a British government were to introduce a Social Charter, it would do so alongside a Bill of Rights, which would include education, as proposed by IPPR.[10] There would be some overlap between provision in the Bill of Rights for 'respect for. . .private and family life' and provision in the Social Charter concerning the right of the family to social, legal and economic protection, but we do not regard this as a problem.

Finally, we include a new proposal for the right to adequate housing: existing provisions of the ESC which impinge on housing are somewhat ambiguous, and have produced little in the way of direct response from the signatory parties.

As a general rule, however, we acknowledge that since the UK is committed to the ESC it follows that the UK should be guided by it in ordering its internal affairs. If the broad terms of the Social Charter of the Council of Europe are considered appropriate for the UK, it would be inconsistent to depart too readily from them in domestic legislation.

We propose adopting Articles 9 to 17 (inclusive) of the European Social Charter, together with Article 4 of the 1988 Protocol. Further proposed additions to the ESC, which have emerged from discussions within the Council of Europe, such as the rights of people with a physical or mental disability, are also included in our draft Charter. We do not at this stage recommend a specific anti-poverty provision, although this clearly has support in some quarters, and is the kind of issue which ought to occupy the attention of the Standing Committee (see below).

The British Social Charter would be an Act of Parliament, passed in the ordinary way without any attempt to entrench it. Entrenching legislation is a difficult business: we would need a written constitution which changed the habits of centuries in order to do so. We leave open the question of whether, in future, a Social Charter might be constitutionally enshrined.

The kind of Charter we propose would be broad in its scope and general in its provisions. Standing alone it would be difficult to interpret intelligently, but it would of course stand alongside existing laws and regulations which refer to such matters as housing, social security, social services and the like. These would, in future, be construed according to provisions of the Social Charter.

We make specific suggestions for legislation on social issues introduced into Parliament after the Charter came into force. As for pre-existing laws and regulations, these would in future fall to be interpreted in the light of the principles embodied in the Charter. Any ambiguity would be resolved in favour of the Charter. In many instances, the Charter would cause past enactments to be interpreted more generously than before.

Anyone seeking to assert rights to social security, for example, would do so in the normal way through social security tribunals, the Social Security Commissioner and the High Court; but any future determination would have to take into account the primary concerns expressed in the Charter. Similarly, someone who sought to compel a public authority to do its duty in relation to the statutory social services, or to homelessness legislation, might do so by applying to the High Court for a judicial review, which is a traditional way of calling government to account. If, say, inadequate social services and community care were provided and no appeal to a special tribunal existed, an order for judicial review would be sought asking that the public body concerned, whether central or local government, carry out its duty. The court would be guided by the Charter in deciding whether a duty had been breached. Parliament would have declared that citizens are entitled to certain basic social rights, and the discretion of public authorities to decide which services to provide and to whom would be circumscribed by the provisions of the Charter.

Since the Charter would have no distinct constitutional status, its provisions could be derogated from by subsequent legislation (though we suggest ways of reducing this likelihood. Legislation would have to be quite specific in its derogations to have the effect of overriding the aims of the Charter. Otherwise, ambiguities would be resolved in favour of the Charter; and more generally, the Charter would be a principal guide to interpreting legislation which impinged on the rights it proclaimed.

It is not possible at this stage to anticipate the many uses to which the Charter might be put, but one example will illustrate its potential influence. We refer to the homelessness legislation. Part III of the Housing Act 1985 deals with the duties which local housing authorities have towards the homeless, and many of its provisions have proved controversial and difficult to interpret constructively. The primary duty extends only to 'priority' cases; 'intentional' homelessness effectively negates the duty; and the authority is obliged to conduct 'such enquiries as are necessary' to determine whether or not someone is homeless. All of these matters (and others) have proved highly contentious. All have presented the courts with formidable problems of interpretation, given their inherent ambiguity (such ambiguities are sometimes introduced deliberately to get support in Parliament for controversial measures). All would, after the passage of the Social Charter, be interpreted subject to the Right to Housing, the Right of the Family to Social, Legal and Economic Protection, and the Right of Mothers and Children to Social and Economic Protection. In cases of ambiguity or doubt, therefore, the larger demands of the Charter could be expected to come into play and, where appropriate, to override earlier case law.

The British Social Charter should include a preamble, which would be an integral part of the legislation and a clear aid to interpretation. This would state that the aims of the Charter are to make every effort to improve the standard of living of all citizens, and to promote the social well-being of both urban and non-urban populations. It would also refer to the requirement to produce the highest standards of health and social welfare, and the right to self-fulfilment and expression.

Enforcing a British Social Charter

We have said that the European Social Charter requires signatory states to furnish information to the Council of Europe on the basis of an extensive and highly detailed *pro forma*. It asks, for example, what preventive measures have been taken by the signatories in relation to certain health hazards such as tobacco, alcohol and AIDS. The provisions of the ESC are thus less general and aspirational than might at first appear. Likewise, a British Social Charter should be accompanied by a Code of Practice or Advice which would be instrumental in interpreting both its own provisions, and those of any discrete legislation where the thrust of the legal obligations was not entirely clear. The Code would be revised from time to time in the light of experience, and subject to the input of the proposed Standing Committee on the Social Charter, to which we now turn.

Given that the Charter would not be entrenched, it is imperative that it be recognised and protected in a way which indicates its special status. To this end, we recommend the establishment of a Standing Advisory Committee on the Social Charter, which would have statutory status and a small permanent secretariat. (This might be seen to represent the social and economic equivalent of the UK Human Rights Commission proposed by IPPR to protect civil and political rights.[11])

It would not be a Parliamentary Committee, but would be more like the Social Security Advisory Committee established under the Social Security Act 1980. It would be a committee of independent experts. It would have a number of functions, all aimed at ensuring that the Social Charter enjoyed a special position in the collective life of the nation. First, the Committee should receive at the earliest possible stage any proposals from Government concerning prospective legislation which might impinge on the concerns expressed in the Charter. It would comment on any possible deleterious effects which the proposals might have in relation to the Charter; the Minister concerned would be under a statutory obligation to make a considered response to these comments, and set these before Parliament. The question remains of how to deal with conflicts of opinion between a Minister and the Committee. One possibility would be to revise the Standing Orders of the two Houses of Parliament to reflect the special status accorded to the deliberations of the Committee. Alternatively, an enhanced role for the Parliamentary Commissioner for Administration might be considered. For example, where the Committee felt that the Minister had not responded satisfactorily to its comments, the Commissioner might be asked to arbitrate.

The Standing Committee would also produce an annual report assessing the impact of the Charter over the previous year and, where necessary, suggesting amendments and reforms to the Charter and its attendant institutions. The report could be expected to assess the record of the Government and Parliament in their support for the Charter, and also of the courts and tribunals in any of their deliberations which impinged on the Charter's provisions. The Committee's report would be addressed to Parliament, and considered by one of the Select Committees of the House of Commons.

Lessons from Europe

It is no small achievement for so many European nations to agree that basic social and economic standards should be observed. Even so, the European Social Charter has had little direct influence. Its provisions, even when formally accepted by individual states, have not always been put into effect in their national legal systems. There are numerous reasons for this, which together amount to a body of problems – persuading us to urge the adoption of a distinctly British Charter based upon the provisions of the ESC. We take the view that a domestic charter would be worth having, even if there were a possibility of strengthening the ESC. But it will be important to build proposals for a British Charter upon experience gained in Europe.

The Council of Europe claims that improvements to legislation, regulations and practices have occurred at a national level as a result of the ESC. Since the Charter came into force in 1965, the Secretariat has been able to register approximately forty changes in national legislation and 'regulations resulting from the Charter'. In the United Kingdom, for example, four areas of improvement were identified by late 1990. However, anyone with experience of British domestic politics would avoid the reductionist view that these had been ineluctably driven by Strasbourg. What effect, if any, the Charter has had in these reforms must remain a matter of speculation.

The position of the UK in relation to most international treaties, including the ESC, is that it will not ratify anything until its domestic laws and/or practices are in line with the treaty in question. This tradition has had its critics but it has also gained praise in the international community. At least they know (or think they know) where the UK stands – and surely this is infinitely preferable to the practice of some states, who will sign every treaty yet have no intention or ability to comply.

Article 20 of the European Social Charter lays down the circumstances under which a contracting party undertakes to consider itself bound and, in order to gain maximum adherence to the Charter, allows for a minimum number of provisions to be accepted while leaving others for future consideration. The UK has, for example, accepted some important provisions of the European Code of Social Security, but has not accepted most of the provisions of Article 12 of the

ESC relating to Social Security. These include paragraphs 2 and 3:

> * to maintain the social-security system at a satisfactory level at least equal to that required for ratification of International Labour Convention (No.102) Concerning Minimum Standards of Social Security; and

> * to endeavour to raise progressively the system of social security to a higher level.

Unlike the European Convention on Human Rights, the ESC has failed to seize the public (or legal) imagination in the UK or elsewhere. Indeed, we have been unable to trace any decided case in the British courts where the European Social Charter has been invoked as an interpretive guide. British jurisprudence takes the view that international treaties, even where ratified, are not part of British domestic law until specifically introduced into our own legal system according to domestic standards and practices. However, it has been a continuous tradition to use our international obligations as an aid to interpretation where British law is in some sense ambiguous. The European Convention on Human Rights has been used in this way on many occasions – although the recent House of Lords decision in R. v Secretary of State for the Home Department, *ex parte* Brind is seen in some quarters as heralding a retreat.[12]

The Council of Europe's Parliamentary Assembly observed in 1977[13] that in its twelfth year of application, the Social Charter remains little known to the public 'in most member states, especially among the sections of the population most concerned'. Little seems to have changed in the intervening period. It is curious that so much attention is currently being paid to the Social Charter of the European Community, while the Council of Europe's Charter remains becalmed.

The Secretariat to the ESC has recently been moved into the Human Rights Secretariat at Strasbourg after many years of comparative isolation. This is evidence of a commitment to the principle that social, economic and cultural rights should be as firmly protected as civil and political rights. In UN debates, the ESC member states have regularly proclaimed the indivisibility of all human rights. Across Europe, concern is being expressed that recent developments require an even greater emphasis to be placed on social rights. Acute social problems have appeared in the countries of Western Europe, and it is hard to forecast the impact of the newly liberalised Eastern European countries joining up with the rest of the international community, not least with the Council of Europe. Furthermore, although we must not elide the Council of Europe and the European Community, the European single market is becoming a source of concern to many interested parties, who are worried lest the market should benefit only the main economic actors. It is worth noting that a working party of EC and EFTA socio-economic interest groups has recently been examining the issue of fundamental social rights – further evidence of the growing interest in social and economic rights within the new Europe.

Since 1989 the Parliamentary Assembly has called for urgent discussion on possible ways of reforming and improving the effectiveness of the ESC.[14] Many believed that a major push towards this goal should be achieved by October 1991, the 30th anniversary of the signing of the Social Charter. In December 1990 the Committee of Ministers' Deputies authorised the convocation of an *ad hoc* Committee charged with making proposals for improving the Social Charter and its operation, particularly the functioning of the supervisory machinery.

The Council of Europe's Parliamentary Assembly has identified major problems in the functioning of the Charter, concerning:

* the respective roles of the Committee of Independent Experts and the Governmental Committee;
* the need to interpret the Charter in a uniform way;
* the fact that no individual recommendations are made by the Committee of Ministers to the states concerned (Article 29 requires a two-thirds majority);
* the disappointing role played by employers' and workers' organisations in the supervision procedure;
* the heavy workload which supervision of the Charter represents for the state authorities and the supervisory bodies;
* the implementation of the procedure relating to unaccepted provisions.

We shall now look in detail at the strengths and weaknesses of the reporting provisions of the ESC. The *pro forma*, on which the signatory parties base their returns to the Council of Europe, is extensive and demanding in terms of information required and the time necessary to secure it. It is an attempt to add teeth to the Charter – and therefore has an important bearing on our proposed Code of Practice. What does it require in relation to the different Articles of the ESC?

On vocational training, for example, each signatory party is asked to indicate, among other things:

* total expenditure from public funds on the vocational guidance service during the last financial year;
* how the arrangements for vocational guidance are divided with reference to the various types of vocational activity;
* what provisions are made for access to higher technical and university education;
* whether, and to what extent, apprenticeships are assisted out of public funds;

      * what measures have been taken to assist adult women wishing to take up work or to resume employment.

When it comes to the protection of health, the *pro forma* requires information on:

      * how health services are made available to the population as a whole;

      * the number of private and public preventive and diagnostic clinics;

      * the number of doctors, dentists, nurses and midwives proportionate to the population, divided where possible between urban and rural areas;

      * protective measures taken in the field of public health such as pollution control and noise abatement;

      * restrictive measures in the campaign against alcoholism and drugs;

      * measures taken to further health education.

Article 16, on the Right of the Family to Social, Legal and Economic Protection, includes protecting family life by such means as social and family benefits, fiscal arrangements, and provisions of family housing benefits for the newly married. The *pro forma* requests information not only on regular and occasional cash benefits, but also on tax reliefs, home-help services, children's holiday homes and the like.

    This is just a flavour of the kind of information required to be reported to Strasbourg. It does suggest that the ESC's rather high-flown and generalistic provisions are intended to be taken seriously: signatory governments are to be called to account for the way they implement their treaty obligations. Whatever the shortcomings of its system of supervision, the Council of Europe clearly regards the provisions of the Social Charter as meaningful and capable of delivering justice in member states.

    The Committee of Experts (COE) attempts to follow the spirit of this belief, in spite of the difficulties under which it operates. A few observations from its conclusions will serve to illustrate the point.[15] The COE has, in recent years, asked governments:

      * to explain the drop in the number of vocational training centres;

      * to provide further information on measures taken to combat drug addiction;

      * to explain apparent anomalies in groups of statistics;

      * to explain the failure to set up day nursery facilities;

      * to provide information on the prevention of and screening for HIV.

It has also noted occasional deterioration in social security benefits, and commented adversely on the absence of a right to appeal against the decisions of bodies responsible for social assistance.

    The UK features relatively rarely in the COE's conclusions. However, having read many volumes of reports from the UK Government, we are bound to say that if the UK is less likely than some other countries to occasion adverse comment, this may have more to do with the sophistication of its responses than with the satisfactory nature of its performance.

One observation regarding the UK is worth expanding upon. In order to determine to what extent the post-1986 Social Security reforms satisfied the requirements of Article 13 (The Right to Social and Medical Assistance), the COE has asked for the next UK report to explain how much total benefit would be received by various types of family in different sets of circumstances under the old and the new systems, and who would be affected by the reduction in the costs of housing benefit. The COE also expressed concern at the restricted rights of appeal, and at cash-limited discretionary benefits previously available as of right. (The response was not available at the time of writing.)

Some Articles have evidently been less effective than others. However, given the form of supervision, little can be done about this. So, for example, the COE has expressed regret that the question of housing for families had received scant attention in the national reports. It has also noted that the Charter's provisions on protecting children and adolescents remain among those which have been least widely accepted; and States which have accepted them have rarely adopted the appropriate measures to rectify shortcomings.[16]

On the other hand, the COE has been able to say that in spite of economic difficulties experienced by signatory states in recent years, social security benefit rates have, for the most part, kept ahead of inflation. It has noted, too, that more countries are giving careful attention to the basic needs of child welfare and the problems in balancing work and family life – although it says more options are needed in the areas of parental leave, part-time work, flexible working hours, childminding facilities and the like. In general, the Committee of Experts appears to entertain a vision of gradually improving standards, with the provisions of the Charter being sufficiently flexible to adapt to changing economic and social conditions.

A principal weakness relates to the information available to the COE upon which it decides how far states have complied with their treaty obligations. The national reports are often ambiguously drafted, sometimes incomplete, and sometimes so swamped with detail that it is impossible for either the secretariat or the COE to make a reasoned judgement. Often, the official versions of events may strike informed and critical observers as highly contentious. But the secretariat does not have sufficient staff to thoroughly digest the documentation it receives.

A body of criticism is developing, to the effect that countervailing or critical evidence is not provided to challenge the official national reports. Our researches have brought this matter to our attention, although most of what we have seen in this respect is presently confidential. Article 23 of the Charter does require the contracting party to submit a copy of its reports to national organisations of employers and trade unions. According to the secretariat of the Council of Europe, these national organisations make little use of the opportunity offered to comment. There is some suggestion that individual governments present voluminous reports to these bodies at the last moment, which naturally makes life exceedingly difficult for them. In any event, the institutional assumption is that the workplace provisions are the ones that really matter – and that is hardly satisfactory from our point of view. Such information as is received from other sources is treated with caution by the COE. At best, it will form the basis for certain questions put to national governments in the next reporting round – but by this time it might well be out of date.

Another weakness lies in the fact that the COE reports via the Governmental Committee to the Parliamentary Assembly of the Council of Europe. The Assembly generally supports the position adopted by the COE and is critical of the Governmental Committee. But the PA, like the Pope, has few battalions. For better or worse, the parliamentary body is less influential than groups of ministers from the member states (as is the case with the EC).

What is most lamentable is the lack of opportunity to cross-examine the reports. Article 27(2) says that the sub-committee of the Governmental Social Committee:

> . . . may consult no more than two representatives of international
> nongovernmental organisations having consultative status with the
> Council of Europe, in respect of questions with which the organisations
> are particularly qualified to deal, such as social welfare, and the
> economic and social protection of the family.

In fact, the Governmental Committee has never enlisted the aid of NonGovernment Organisations (NGOs) on such matters. Those NGOs which are accorded status within the Council of Europe (and there are very few from the UK) have been understandably critical about the supervisory system. At the NGO meeting in the Council of Europe in January 1991, a joint statement underlined the necessity of giving fresh impetus to the ESC, and stressed in particular the need to widen the sources of information available to the supervisory bodies.

There is a provision in Article 22 for commissioning reports on non-accepted provisions. This has been invoked three times since the Charter came into force; at this rate it would take about sixty years to consider all the provisions which have not been accepted. This means there is little incentive for parties to accept further provisions, and no chance at all for the Committee to gain a comprehensive and up-to-date picture of the situation in the contracting states.

There are numerous suggestions in train for reform of the ESC, and we could add a list of our own. A limited right of individual petition might be particularly useful: to allow NGOs or individuals to complain about the conduct of their government in relation to the accepted provisions of the Charter, and to request a ruling on the basis of information supplied or gathered. It remains to be seen how much support this suggestion attracts. In general, it is extremely difficult to persuade a large group of sovereign states to act in harmony, especially on the social and economic front. We therefore contend that it is time for the UK to put its own house in order. This requires reform of domestic law.

The reform must be firmly based upon the ESC, though we suggest some refinements. Experience gained with the Charter over the years offers important guidelines, not least about the kind of information that should be sought through the reporting procedure. The palpable failure of housing policies has alerted us to the need for stronger provision on this front; and we are guided by the COE's observation that few countries have accepted the ESC's provisions on protecting children and adolescents. We also have no doubt that the 'improvement formula' of Article 12(3) needs clear endorsement in a domestic charter, so that a firm commitment is made 'to raise progressively the system of social security to a higher level'.

Perhaps the final lesson from the ESC concerns the relationship between the public and the private sectors. It is now commonplace to observe the blurring of the line between the state and the private sectors.[17] Responsibilities for economic and social provision have increasingly been farmed out by the state in the last decade. In order to reveal the true picture of conformity to basic standards, attention must therefore be paid not only to state provision, but also to para-state and partnership arrangements as well as to the private sector itself. This is occasionally referred to in the ESC[18] but is brought out more forcefully in the reporting *pro forma*. For example, in relation to Article 14(2) regarding the right to benefit from social welfare services, information is requested about the encouragement, financial and otherwise, to voluntary work in the social services field. In the field of health, information is required about the proportions of public and private establishments and their specialisms, as well as on the level of private funds devoted to providing medical assistance. What is made clear is that however wide the range of sources from which provisions are made, it is the responsibility of government to ensure that the total package is adequate. Such information must be made available and accessible to the institutions with executive and supervisory responsibility under a British Social Charter.

The next section indicates the kinds of provision we believe could form the basis of a British Social Charter. References are made, where appropriate, to the relevant Article of the ESC or part of the European Code of Social Security (ECofSS), upon which each section is based. Some of these have been adapted, others remain unchanged.

We have not included specific proposals for the Code of Practice. Many features of the ESC *pro forma* ought to be included, but this should be the subject of extensive debate, taking into account the lessons from Europe outlined above. Codes are, of course, flexible and can move with the times. The British system of social justice ought to be a dynamic process, aided by a new Social Charter and its accompanying Code which can be adapted and improved from time to time.

A draft charter of social rights

Preamble

Recognising our Treaty obligations under the European Social Charter and the European Code of Social Security of the Council of Europe.

Recognising that the aim of our policy is to make every effort to improve the standard of living of all citizens and to promote the social well-being of both the urban and non-urban populations.

Recognising that our aim is also to produce the highest standards of health and social welfare and the right to self-fulfilment and expression.

Recognising that the enjoyment of social rights should be secured without discrimination on grounds of race, colour, sex, religion, political opinion, national extraction or social origin.

The Queen in Parliament hereby enacts:

Part One

Section 1: The right to protection of health (Article 11 ESC)

The Government undertakes, either directly or in co-operation with public or private organisations, to take appropriate measures designed, *inter alia*: to remove as far as possible the causes of ill-health; to provide advisory and educational facilities for the promotion of health and the encouragement of individual responsibility in matters of health; to prevent as far as possible epidemic, endemic and other diseases.

Section 2: The right to medical care (Article 11 EC of SS)

(1) The Government undertakes to secure the provision of services in respect of a condition requiring medical care, which shall include the following:

(a) general practitioner care, including domiciliary visiting;

(b) specialist care at hospitals for in-patients and out-patients, and such specialist care as may be available outside hospitals;

(c) the essential pharmaceutical supplies as prescribed by medical or other qualified practitioners;

(d) hospitalisation, where necessary;

(e) in case of pregnancy and confinement and their consequences, prenatal, confinement and post-natal care either by medical practitioners or by qualified midwives, and hospitalisation where necessary.

(2) The services provided in accordance with this section shall be afforded with a view to maintaining, restoring or improving the health of the person protected and his/her ability to work and to attend to his/her personal needs.

(3) Those protected by these services shall be encouraged to avail themselves of the health services placed at their disposal.

Section 3: The right to social security (Article 12 ESC)

The Government undertakes to maintain a system of social security at a satisfactory level at least equal to that required for ratification of the European Code of Social Security, and to endeavour to raise progressively the system of social security to a higher level.

Section 4: The right to social and medical assistance (Article 13 ESC)

(1) The Government undertakes to ensure that any person who is without adequate resources and who is unable to secure such resources either by his/her own efforts or from other sources, in particular by benefits under a social security scheme, be granted adequate assistance and, in case of sickness, the care necessitated by his/her condition.

(2) Such persons receiving such assistance shall not, for that reason, suffer from a diminution of their political or social rights.

(3) It is also provided that everyone may receive by appropriate public or private services such advice and personal help as may be required to prevent, to remove, or to alleviate personal or family want.

Section 5: The right to benefit from social welfare services (Article 14 ESC)

(1) The Government undertakes to promote or provide services which, by using methods of social work, would contribute to the welfare and development of both individuals and groups in the community, and to their adjustment to the social environment.

(2) Individuals and voluntary or other organisations are to be encouraged to participate in the establishment and maintenance of such services.

Section 6: The right to vocational guidance (Article 9 ESC)

The Government undertakes to provide or promote, as necessary, a service which will assist all persons, including those with disabilities, to solve problems related to occupational choice and progress, with due regard to the individual's characteristics and their relation to occupational opportunity: this assistance should be available free of charge, both to young persons, including school children, and to adults.

Section 7: The right to vocational training (Article 10 ESC)

(1) The Government undertakes to provide or promote, as necessary, the technical and vocational training of all persons, including those with disabilities, in consultation with employers' and workers' organisations, and to grant facilities for access to higher technical and university education, based solely on individual aptitude.

(2) There shall be provided or promoted a system of apprenticeship or other systematic arrangements for training young boys and girls in their various employments.

(3) There shall be provided or promoted, as necessary, adequate and readily available training facilities for adult workers, and special facilities for the re-training of adult workers needed as a result of technological development or new trends in employment.

(4) There shall be encouragement of the full utilisation of the facilities provided, by appropriate measures such as reducing or abolishing any fees or charges; granting financial assistance in appropriate cases; including in the normal working hours time spent on supplementary training taken by the worker, at the request of his/her employer, during employment.

(5) There shall be ensured, through adequate supervision, in consultation with employers' and workers' organisations, the efficiency of apprenticeship and other training arrangements for young workers, and the adequate protection of young workers generally.

Section 8: The right of physically or mentally disabled persons to vocational training, rehabilitation and social resettlement (Article 15 ESC)

The Government undertakes to take adequate measures for the provision of training facilities, including, where necessary, specialised institutions, public or private, and to take adequate measures for the placing of disabled persons in employment, such as specialised placing services, facilities for sheltered employment and measures to encourage employers to admit disabled persons to employment.

Section 9: The right of the family to social, legal and economic protection (Article 16 ESC, Part VII ECofSS)

The Government undertakes to promote the economic, legal and social protection of family life by such means as social and family benefits, fiscal arrangements, provision of family housing, financial or other benefits for families with children, and other appropriate means.

Section 10: The right of mothers and children to social and economic protection (Article 17 ESC)

The Government undertakes to take all appropriate and necessary measures to ensure the effective exercise of the right of mothers and children to social and economic protection, including the establishment or maintenance of appropriate institutions or services.

Section 11: The right of elderly persons to social protection (Article 4 Protocol ESC)

(1) The Government undertakes to adopt or encourage, either directly or in co-operation with public or private organisations, appropriate measures designed in particular to enable elderly persons to remain full members of society for as long as possible, by means of adequate resources enabling them to lead a decent life and play an active part in public, social and cultural life, and the provision of information about services and facilities available for elderly persons and their opportunities to make use of them.

(2) Elderly persons shall also be enabled to choose their life-style freely and to lead independent lives in their familiar surroundings for as long as they wish and are able, by means of provision of housing suited to their needs and their state of health or of adequate support for adapting their housing, and the health care and the services necessitated by their state.

(3) Elderly persons living in institutions shall also be guaranteed appropriate support, while respecting their privacy, and participation in decisions concerning living conditions in the institution.

Section 12: The right to old-age benefit (Part V ECofSS)

All persons above the age of 60 shall be entitled to a pension, except that such payment may be reduced by prescribed amounts in the case of a person being engaged in gainful activity.

Section 13: The right to housing

All persons shall be entitled to adequate housing provision according to their circumstances. In interpreting this provision the need to keep the family unit intact shall be of pre-eminent importance.

Part Two

Section 14

(1) All legislative provisions in force before the passing of this Act shall, after the

coming into force of this Act, be interpreted so as to give effect, wherever possible, to its provisions.

(2) All publicly exercised discretion affecting any matters which relate to the subject matter of this Act shall be exercised so as to give effect, wherever possible, to its provisions.

(3) All legislative provisions introduced after the passage of this Act shall be interpreted so as to give effect, wherever possible, to its provisions unless an Act of the United Kingdom Parliament expressly provides to the contrary.

Section 15

(1) On an appointed day the Secretary of State shall establish a Standing Advisory Committee on the Social Charter (the Committee) whose members shall be appointed according to terms and conditions laid down by statutory instrument introduced by the Secretary of State subject to the affirmative resolution of the House of Commons.

(2) The functions of the Committee shall include the following:

> *(a)* Receiving, at the earliest possible stage, any proposals from the Government concerning matters which are likely to impinge on the provisions of Part One of this Act.

> *(b)* Commenting on any proposals envisaged in (a) above. Where the Committee considers that such proposals would or might detract from the provisions of Part One of this Act, the Secretary of State shall be obliged to respond to the Committee's comments within 30 days, such response to be laid upon the table of the House of Commons.

> *(c)* Producing an annual report on its work, including an assessment of the impact of the Charter over the previous year, including the conduct of Ministers of the Crown, their agents and intermediaries, including non-departmental public bodies, the courts and tribunals. The report shall be laid before both Houses of Parliament. From time to time, the Committee may make periodic reports covering either a shorter or longer period than one year where it deems it desirable.

Section 16

(1) On an appointed day the Secretary of State shall lay before both Houses of Parliament a Code of Practice concerning the provisions of Part One of this Act after consulting with parties appearing to him to be interested, including the Committee. The Secretary of State shall be empowered to amend the Code from time to time, providing that he engages in a similar degree of consultation.

(2) In interpreting the provisions of Part One of this Act, the appropriate court,

tribunal, Minister of the Crown or representative of the Minister shall have regard to the provisions of the Code.

Conclusion

Elsewhere in this volume, the philosophical case has been made out for social rights to take their place alongside civil and political rights. It is worth adding that social rights are necessary for self-fulfilment and expression. It is difficult to express one's personality if one is economically deprived. The security of physical well being is a prerequisite of emotional well being.

It is remarkable that so little is known about the European Social Charter. Yet the UK is a signatory to most of its provisions and has been for many years. It seems logical to us therefore to give domestic force to ideas which are already endorsed by solemn and binding undertakings with international allies.

Traditionally, the British have taken the view that rights can be left to the political marketplace. This belongs to the school of thought that says Britain does not need a constitution, since all the decent things a constitution would require are already being done. Such arguments disregard the complexity of modern politics and the modern world. For instance, few serious observers now believe that the doctrine of ministerial responsibility is a source of real accountability in modern conditions. It is, instead, used as an obstacle to all but insiders obtaining information and access to the decision-making process. Nor is it possible to believe, given the power of the modern executive, that the common law contains its own charter of values and rights. The British constitution has no checks and balances: no check on the executive; nothing to tip the balance of power towards the citizen. Furthermore, the last decade has seen a considerable accumulation of power at the centre. So the question must be put: should the basic conditions of citizenship be protected?

If the answer is yes, it is hard to know how this can be done without giving a special status in law to fundamental principles. These must surely now include the basic social and economic rights. The question that remains is how these basic rights are to be expressed. We take the view that, since the UK is already committed to the European Social Charter, then that should form the core of a domestic charter. It will have more force than the ESC, if a supervisory system is devised for it which builds on lessons learned in Strasbourg, if it becomes a means for interpreting existing legislation and if it provides guidance for the framing of future laws and regulations. Under these conditions, it could play a role of considerable importance in the coming years.

In the early 1990s there has been much talk of citizens' charters, and we shall no doubt hear more. We contend that concern about the specifics of service delivery should not overshadow the need to establish the basic preconditions of a happy life – and that these involve social and economic, no less than civil and political, rights. Our proposals for a British Social Charter are an attempt to fuel a debate on this subject – the need for which becomes increasingly urgent.

3 PROCEDURAL RIGHTS IN SOCIAL WELFARE

Denis Galligan

The ultimate test of any welfare system is how well it satisfies people's needs. Where resources are limited, policy choices should be made about the relative importance of different welfare needs and those policies implemented through the allocation of resources. What constitutes a fair allocations policy and how such policies are to be arrived at are political questions of fundamental importance which raise interesting issues about the procedures appropriate to policy-making. However, no matter how good or bad the policies may be, decisions have to be made as to whether individual claimants are eligible for a particular benefit or service, or whether individuals might be required to receive a service. There are, in other words, always two levels of decision-making: one to settle the policies, the other to translate those policies into decisions about individuals. It is with the latter that we are concerned in this chapter.

Making decisions about individuals can involve addressing a wide range of questions: whether a person qualifies for a service; what service exactly is required; how long the service should continue; whether a service should be provided to one person rather than another, and so on. These are just a few examples of the kinds of decision entailed in implementing policies. They are often made by officials and practitioners working under pressure, with limited knowledge, sometimes with inadequate training, and almost always against a backdrop of scarce resources. Moreover, while broad policy decisions are made in the abstract, decisions about individuals are made in a personal context. Each decision is about how one particular person is to be treated. Between the decision-maker and the claimant there is a relationship, in some ways a personal transaction; decisions within that relationship must steer a hazardous course between the unique and subjective needs of the person on the one hand, and the need to maintain general and objective standards on the other.

It is against this setting that questions of procedure arise. Procedures are necessary to ensure that decisions which apply policies to individual cases are made in a way that is effective, economical, and timely. That is by no means a mechanical task; decisions involve judgement, discretion, even speculation, and procedures are needed to guide and regulate that process. Procedures are also necessary to ensure that the correct information is available and that professional opinions are reliable. Another task of procedures is to provide avenues for the claimant or recipient to complain about the way he or she has been treated or considered by an authoritative body.

The main task of procedures, however, is to ensure that the individual claimant is treated fairly. Fairness is a complex and variable notion, but there are certain basic aspects of fairness, which can loosely be referred to as procedural fairness, and which are fundamental to any acceptable course of decision-making. The main object of this chapter is to develop that notion of procedural fairness in the context of welfare services.

The object of procedures and notions of fairness

There are two elements in a full understanding of procedural fairness. The first is linked to outcomes, and the need to have procedures which lead to the right outcomes. The second element is separate from outcomes, and is based on values about how individuals should be treated in the making of decisions affecting them. I shall examine each of these in turn.

Fairness in relation to outcomes

The primary object of procedures is to lead to satisfactory outcomes. What amounts to a satisfactory outcome depends on the objects and purposes of each area of decision-making. The general object of all welfare decisions is to provide the appropriate services to those who need them. However, within specific contexts, that general purpose will be achieved through objects and policies of a more precise kind.

An essential element in the concept of procedural fairness is that procedures are fair if they lead to the correct outcome. The basis of fairness in this sense is twofold. For the one part, the fairness of the procedure flows from the justice of the outcome; if the policies governing the distribution of welfare are themselves just, then procedures conducive to those outcomes are also to that extent fair. This sense of fairness is of course always open to the objection that the fairness of the procedures is totally dependent on the substantive justice of the outcome. Whether the outcome is just depends on the values and policies being implemented. The fairness of procedures, in this sense, like the justice of outcomes, is variable.

The second part to this sense of fairness is that procedures which produce the right outcomes by applying the governing legal rules and standards, thereby show that those rules and standards are to be taken seriously. By passing laws and delegating authority to officials and administrative bodies, society determines how certain issues are to be dealt with. Having decided in this way, fairness requires that such rules and standards be upheld. On the basis of these structures, expectations are created, and such expectations are to be respected. This goes to the heart of a legal system; legal rules and standards might not be perfect, but they do provide some certainty and predictability as to how important social issues are to be resolved. As Bentham argued in the nineteenth century and as others have repeated since, stability and continuity are important features of a tolerable society. On this basis it can be seen that the even application of legal standards satisfies a sense of fairness. Accordingly, procedures which lead to that end are in that sense fair.

There are, however, certain difficulties in applying this first sense of procedural fairness to welfare decisions. A notable characteristic of this area is the *high level of discretion*. Discretion is another concept which has various meanings and connotations, but generally it suggests an area of choice in decision-making.[1] The standards governing decisions may be expressed in broad and general terms, leaving it to the decision makers to render them more precise. There may be different standards which are in conflict and pull in different directions, so that in the course of decisions, choices have to be made as to their relative weight and importance. Discretion may also allow for different factors to be taken into account, where the relative weight of each is left to the decisionmaker's judgement. Even though the standards are clear in themselves, their application to actual situations may allow extensive freedom of judgement. In short, it is often the case in welfare decisions that there is no right decision in any objective sense; the task rather is left to the provider to reach the decision which, in all the circumstances, seems to be best.

How then does procedural fairness, in the instrumental sense of producing correct outcomes, apply in the context of discretion? The answer is that, although there may not be one correct outcome, it is reasonable to expect an outcome which satisfies a number of other values. The ideas of *reason and non-arbitrariness* point to what is required – for example:

* discretionary decisions should be based on a firm foundation of facts and evidence;
* all relevant matters should be taken into account, including the particular circumstances of the claimant or complainant;
* the governing standards should be interpreted reasonably;
* reasons should be given which show how the final decision is explained and justified.

These ideas can be taken further – thus:

* discretion should be structured through the adoption of guidelines and more specific policies;
* provision should be made for enabling the complainant to be involved in the decision, at least to the extent of knowing the case to

be met or the conditions to be satisfied, and being able to submit
evidence and argument.

Certain values shape the way decisions are to be made. Where the decision
depends on the application of a clear rule, the main concern is to apply the rule
accurately; the values served are certainty and predictability. As decisions move
away from that towards a more discretionary position, certainty and
predictability still have a place, but other values, based on reason, purpose and
non-arbitrariness come into play. The more clearly a decision measures up to
those values, the more likely it is to be considered fair. The test of good and fair
procedures is whether they lead to decisions of that kind.

The underlying notion is *legitimate authority*: in order for decisions to be
legitimate and acceptable, they must comply with certain values which the
community holds to be important. Procedural fairness is closely associated with
the realisation of those values in decision-making.

We now have the first sense of procedural fairness: it is linked to outcomes
and to the values which in turn shape those outcomes.

Fair procedures and respect for persons

The second element of fair procedures derives from the idea *that individuals
should be treated with dignity and respect* in decisions affecting them. Fairness in
this sense is not attached to outcomes of a particular kind, but requires that
certain values be upheld in the decision-making process. These 'process values'
may derive from various sources, but one of the central principles derives from
the idea of dignity and respect. This in turn is often linked to the Kantian
principle that individuals should be treated as ends in themselves, not as the
means to other ends.[2] The principle might also be based on the notion of a social
compact between the members of a society. A fundamental term of such a
compact might be that, in all activities of law and government, individuals and
their interests are important and count in any decisions about the allocation of
benefits and burdens.

The principles deriving from values such as dignity and respect are
independent of outcomes, and apply to all forms of decision-making where the
interests of individuals are at stake. They constitute a framework into which all
decisions must pass, if they are to be justifiable. So, for example, the principle
that a person should be heard before a decision is made about him is regarded as
a fundamental requirement of fairness. That principle is held to be important
because it is said to derive from the notion of treating people with respect. A
similar argument would support the case for other procedures, such as giving
reasons for decisions; a person should be told why the decision has been made to
treat him or her in a particular way. By contrast, procedures instrumental to

outcomes would apply the hearing principle, or other procedures, only insofar as each contributed to a better outcome. Now of course the same procedure might be justified both for its role in producing good outcomes and for its link to process values.

We cannot here venture into the deeper philosophical issues which lie behind the different senses of procedural fairness. But two brief comments should be made. First, the relationship between procedures and outcomes depends very much on the nature of different decisions and the context in which they are made. However, the question in any context will be which procedures are most likely to lead to the best outcomes. Second, philosophers do argue about the nature of process values, and indeed about which values ought to have a place in decision-making. They also argue about what particular values require in terms of procedures. For example, does the principle of treating people with respect require that they be given a hearing in all situations where they might be affected? However, as we shall see shortly, while philosophical debate goes on, some of these issues have been settled within the law.[3]

To sum up then, procedural fairness turns on two important ideas. The first is that a person, whether claimant or complainant, should be treated in accordance with the law; that means reaching decisions according to the requirements and values of the law. Procedures must be designed to ensure that people are, in that sense, treated properly. The second idea is that there are other values to be taken into account, values which are independent of particular outcomes, but which derive from the moral and philosophical understandings of a particular society.

Basic principles of procedural fairness

Ideas of procedural fairness are fairly well developed in the modern legal system of the United Kingdom. The formulation of procedural principles has traditionally been left to the courts, although in recent years Parliament, through legislation, has shown a greater interest. The passing of the Police and Criminal Evidence Act 1984 and the codes of practice which accompany it, mark one notable case of a legislative attempt to set out a code of procedures. The procedural provisions of the Tribunals and Inquiries Act is another. In general, however, innovation and development are left to the courts, and since the courts rule only on matters that come before them, the development of a jurisprudence of procedures is bound to be piecemeal and uneven.

Nevertheless, in the last thirty years the courts have done much to develop principles of fair procedures which are suitable to the judicial trial and which also apply to the great variety of decisions made by officials in the exercise of governmental or quasi-governmental powers. But the law is slow to move and in many respects is incomplete. In general, however, since the courts rule only on matters that come before them, the development of a jurisprudence of procedures is bound to be piecemeal and uneven. In the next section, therefore, I set out not only the principles which are firmly based in English law, but also those principles which merit adoption, and whose adoption would be compatible with existing principles.

Most principles can be justified both in terms of their contribution to outcomes and in terms of process values. However, in the following account, the question of justification for each principle is not addressed.

The hearing principle

The first and most fundamental principle is that a person should be heard before a decision is made against his or her interests. This means that those subject to or affected by the decision should be told the case against them, or more appropriately in the welfare field, should be told the criteria that have to be met and the facts that have to be established, and be given the opportunity to present evidence and argument. In English law this principle is referred to as the first principle of natural justice. Its origins are found in the criminal trial, but in recent years it has been extended to cover many forms of administrative decision-making.

The hearing principle applies whenever a person has significant rights or interests affected by the decision or, alternatively, when expectations arise that there will be a hearing before a decision is taken. Once that principle applies, the next question is what sort of hearing is required. This may range from a full oral hearing at one end of the spectrum to written representations at the other end. What form of hearing is required depends largely on the nature of the decision, the importance of the interests at stake, and the consequences for those interests.

Absence of bias

The second fundamental principle of procedural fairness is that there should be no bias on the part of the decision-maker. Bias is an interesting concept, and may include a number of possibilities: for example, bias against the person subject to the decision, or bias in the sense of personal gain or advantage to the decision-maker. It might also include a more subtle sense of bias, where the decision-maker is committed to a particular policy or approach, and is not prepared to depart from it, whatever the circumstances. This last sense of bias is hard to establish, and some line has to be drawn between having settled policies and yet being prepared to consider each case on its merits.

Equality and consistency

The next principle is that people should be treated with equality and consistency.

A notion of equality before the law is fundamental to the very idea of an orderly and equitable society. A similar idea applies in the distribution of burdens and benefits generally. In crude terms, this means that people claiming or being subjected to welfare services should be treated with equality. At its most fundamental, this principle forbids factors extraneous to the question of welfare being taken into account: if the issue is whether welfare should be provided to a particular person, then, only matters such as need and availability, which are rationally relevant, should be considered. Extraneous factors such as colour, sex, age, or ethnic origins would simply be irrelevant.

At another level, the principle of equal treatment requires equality in a more positive sense. If A gets a benefit, then in similar circumstances B should get the same benefit. The reasons which support giving the benefit to A are also good reasons for giving it to B. Similarly, when a policy is laid down as to how certain situations are to be dealt with, it should be applied even-handedly to all who come within it.

While the principle is easy enough to state, it is not so easy to apply. Whether two situations or sets of circumstances are the same can be a difficult matter of judgement, which may depend on the outlook and approach of the person making the judgement. Moreover, there has to be room for change and progress; policies must not be too rigid, and indeed policies may need to be changed. The mere fact that cases have been dealt with in a particular way in the past should not hinder a different and better approach in the future. It may be that inadequacies in existing policies become apparent only in the course of considering a particular set of circumstances. These qualifications do not detract from the importance of the general principle that people should be treated equally and consistently; that is fundamental. But the principle is complex both philosophically and in practical application. Its precise content requires careful thought and analysis in each context of decision making.

Structured discretion

The fourth principle concerns the structuring of discretion. This means the formulation of guidelines as to how different powers will be exercised. Guidelines can take the form of policy statements, internal rules, directives, even opinions. The underlying principle is that structuring leads to better and fairer decisions.[4] Guidelines encourage consistency in decisions; they may also encourage a more reflective attitude on the part of decision-makers, both in formulating guidelines and in keeping them under review. Guidelines are helpful in reviewing decisions; individual cases can be tested against the guidelines. The very idea of guidelines suggests that they will not be applied inflexibly; but where there are departures, reasons should be given. This would justify the specific decision and may point to the need for change in the general guideline.

The structuring principle can also be linked to the hearing principle. In order to make the hearing principle worthwhile, it is necessary to know the criteria being used. Guidelines which are formulated and publicised go a long way towards meeting that requirement.

It should also be noted that the structuring of discretion can be applied both to matters of policy and to professional judgement. This may at first seem surprising. While there is no difficulty about expressing policies in guidelines and directions, the very nature of professional judgement seems to depend on applying specialist knowledge to particular facts. Such a process, it is often claimed, cannot be reduced to guidelines. There is, of course, truth in that claim, but the immunity of professional judgement from guidelines is easily overstated. Two general points should be kept in mind:

First, elements of policy are prone to be concealed under the cloak of expert or specialist judgement. In order to avoid that situation, any claim of immunity should be closely analysed. Second, even within the scope of expert judgement, many aspects become routinised and standardised. Not every case that arises is unique; indeed, most cases fall into readily identifiable patterns. There is no good reason for not trying to identify recurring situations and problems, and bringing them within a framework of guidelines, subject always to the discretion of the official to depart from those guidelines, if professional judgement in the particular case so requires.

Finally, a note of caution.[5] Although structuring is fundamental to the proper administration of a system of welfare, it has its pitfalls. There is a tendency for guidelines to be applied rigidly in cases which might require a more flexible approach. The optimum balance between guidelines and open discretion always requires careful judgement and planning. Guidelines have a tendency to ossify; they can also become shields behind which the providers of welfare can hide, and in that way avoid difficult decisions and personal responsibility. Moreover, some complex matters do not easily lend themselves to general guidelines; to force them into guidelines may remove a necessary flexibility of action. However, these are notes of caution, they are not arguments against the general need for guidelines.

The following doctrines relating to guidelines in exercising discretion are established in law:

* guidelines may be formulated, but there is no positive duty to do so;
* where there are guidelines, they must not be applied rigidly, but account must be taken of the merits of the particular case;
* if guidelines are laid down, the law tends to require that they be applied consistently to cases that come within them;
* guidelines can be changed at any time.

Reasons for decisions

The next principle of procedural fairness is that reasons for decisions should be given. The duty to give reasons may improve the quality of the decision. It is important also in helping the person affected to understand the decision and perhaps recognise its validity. The giving of reasons also provides the basis for an appeal or review of the decision. Generally, the giving of reasons is considered fundamental to procedural fairness.

One difficulty is to determine what counts as adequate reasons. There may be a temptation to explain a decision in terms of a safe formula which does not really address the specific situation. What counts as adequate will again depend on the situation, but it would normally be required to state the following:

* the facts of the case;
* the guidelines or other criteria being applied;
* how the present case fails within the criteria; or,
* if the criteria have been departed from, the reasons for departure.

While the need for reasons is rarely questioned, the law on this point lags seriously behind. There is no general duty at common law on an official, or quasi-official, to state the reasons for a decision. There are, however, extensive statutory duties on many public bodies to give reasons, and a body of law has developed as to what constitute adequate reasons. The general tendency is for Parliament to impose a duty to give reasons when creating new authorities, or when regulating an area of activity for the first time.

Complaints and appeals

The final procedural principle is that provision be made for complaints and appeals. The underlying idea is that a person should have a reasonable opportunity to have the actions and decisions of one official reviewed by another. Again there is enormous scope for different types of review and appeal, but the principle itself is entrenched in law and practice.

While these principles are basic to procedural fairness, they are not comprehensive and others might be added. For example, access to information, and knowledge of the rights and procedure available, are vital matters if the system is to work effectively and fairly.

To sum up. The theoretical basis of procedural fairness has been examined, and the specific principles have been identified and analysed. While each is clear enough in theory, the application in practice is greatly influenced by the actual context. However, it is necessary to clarify the principles before trying to settle the practice.

Procedural rights

The discussion so far has been in terms of procedural fairness, but now we must consider the question of procedural rights. In general terms, to have a right is to have a justifiable claim against the community that a particular interest be given a certain recognition or protection. This approach is often referred to as the interest theory of rights; rights are simply protected interests.[6] Of course not all interests are protected as rights; the actual rights are dependent on a particular context. Here we are concerned with legal rights, and so we must look to the legal system. Within any legal system, certain interests will be considered to be sufficiently important to justify special protection. Where there is such a protected interest, duties will normally be imposed on others to respect those special interests and to treat them in particular ways. For this reason it is often said that duties are correlative to rights. Legal rights are normally protected by providing for the legal enforcement of the correlative duties.

Although we usually think of rights in terms of substantive benefits, procedural rights have a vital role. It is part of the very idea of a substantive right that procedures be available to secure it. In welfare this means that where there are rights to certain benefits, there are procedural rights to the means necessary to obtain those benefits.[7]

There are, however, many situations in welfare where there is no right to a particular outcome, but rather a provider's discretion to consider whether the benefit should be granted. Such decisions must strive to consider the case, to take all relevant matters into account, and to reach a decision which is rational, purposive, and non-arbitrary. It can be claimed with some persuasion that the applicant has a right to a decision which meets those criteria, and accordingly has a further right to the procedures which will ensure an outcome of that kind.

There is another basis for procedural rights in relation to those 'process values', such as dignity and respect, which were referred to above. If a person is entitled to be treated with dignity and respect, then it follows that he is also entitled to procedures which will ensure treatment in that way. The claimant has, in other words, procedural rights both to ensure that correct decisions are reached and to ensure that he or she is treated with dignity and respect.

Procedures and costs

There are various costs involved in the provision of procedures.[8] The first and most obvious are the *direct costs* of providing institutions, personnel, facilities, etc., necessary for the effective operation of the system. Those costs can be substantial.

A second category of costs can be referred to as *social costs*; that is, the cost – or waste – incurred in failing to achieve the objects and purposes of the enterprise. These take two forms. One is the overall cost to the community in not achieving effectively the objects for which resources have been given. The other is the cost to the individual in terms of disappointment and frustration in not getting the service or benefit expected.

A third area of cost has been referred to as *moral costs*: the costs of treating a person unfairly. In addition to the cost of failing to achieve the objects of the decision, this is the cost of wrongly depriving the person of a service to which he or she has a right. There can also be a moral cost in failing to have or to follow fair procedures. The basis of moral costs is unfair treatment.[9]

A welfare system should try to keep to a minimum all three types of cost, but generally there will be competition between direct costs on the one hand, and social and moral costs on the other hand. The general task is to find an acceptable accommodation between them.

In devising procedures for the provision of welfare, the argument has to be made that, for an outlay of reasonably modest direct costs, substantial gains can be made in social and moral costs for an outlay of reasonably modest direct costs. Although some direct costs will be necessary, by way of better procedures, the levels of effectiveness and efficiency, normally, can be improved significantly. A better system for hearing complaints and appeals will remove some of the social costs in bad decision-making, and in the levels of frustration suffered by people seeking services. Regular review of the system's operation will also help in making it more effective. Any improvement in procedures will generally reduce the moral costs resulting from unsatisfactory outcomes and an appearance of unfairness. The main point is that the direct costs of better procedures are often more than offset by the reduction in social and moral costs.

Special features of welfare

The provision of welfare has some particular features which bear upon procedures:

* The *resources are severely limited* in relation to the demands, with the result that many claims may have to be rejected or met only partly.
* There is *substantial discretion* at all levels of decision-making. That discretion is often left to the decision-makers without clear guidelines. Principles and strategies for regulating discretion are therefore especially important here.
* Questions of *policy and professional judgement are often merged or confused*. The relationship between the two is complex, but two general points should be noted. First, the distinction between the two should be kept as clear as possible. Second, as we saw earlier, both

matters can be the subject of guidelines and directions.

* There is an *understandable reluctance to spend on procedures* scarce resources devoted to welfare. The more spent on procedures, the less available for substantive services. However, the discussion of costs above shows that better procedures should make the system of distribution more effective, and in that way actually improve the level of distribution.

* Those who need welfare services are often (not always) at a *particular disadvantage associated with sickness, disability, poverty, extreme youth or old age.* There are two likely consequences: firstly, they often suffer the additional handicap of being regarded by others, including welfare providers, as incompetent or sub-normal – in other words, they are not afforded the dignity and respect which ought to be the right of every human being. Secondly, many have unreasonably low expectations about what is due to them, arising from a lack of opportunity to develop or maintain self-esteem, or to discover what might be available. Procedures are therefore needed to ensure that all citizens have access to information about services and procedures, with appropriate help for those who need it, to secure information, to utilise procedures, and to gain access to services.

* The sense of *grievance and frustration* felt by those caught up in the system is likely to be acute. Procedures which ensure that all cases are considered and decided fairly, and which make adequate provision for the hearing of grievances and appeals, may help to alleviate this problem.

* Although welfare is usually seen as distributing services to those who need them, it can also be *forced on involuntary recipients.* In that sense, the provision of welfare is analogous to the imposition of sanctions, and accordingly there should be procedural protections appropriate to that kind of decision.

Applying procedures to welfare

A full sense of procedural principles in welfare can be developed around the following:

(1) Informing claimants of the services available.

(2) Getting claims before the providers and decision-makers.

(3) Ensuring expedition in deciding cases.

(4) Dealing with individual cases, in particular:

   * the formulation and publication of guidelines as to how cases will be dealt with, orally or in writing;

* the opportunity to put one's case before the decision-maker, whether
* the availability to both provider and claimant of facts and other
material relevant to the issue, including the reports and opinions of
experts;
* impartiality on the part of the provider;
* consistency in treatment and equality in distribution;
* a statement of reasons for each decision, including the facts, the
criteria, and an explanation of how the one has been applied to the
other.

(5) Periodic review of the circumstances of claimants and the appropriateness of provision previously agreed.

(6) Providing for appeal against decisions made, in particular:
* making known the ground for appeal;
* initial review, within the relevant agency, of factors relevant to the
decision;
* provision for the more investigative functions of an ombudsman, who
should have the power to make recommendations not only about the
individual case but also about more general issues.

(7) Providing for complaints to be heard about the quality of service provided, in particular:
* specification of services and standards;
* investigation and resolution within the agency;
* provision for appeal against the outcomes of the agency's internal
review to an independent body;
* provision for independent review and investigation.

(8) Criteria for and modes of redress.

These points are developed further in the next chapter.

Conclusion

It is always tempting to think of procedures as technical matters of little interest or importance. What really matters, after all, is the end result, not the means for reaching it. Finally, it is of course true that the test of a good system is whether it produces good results. But to imagine that good results are separate from good procedures would be a serious mistake. Indeed, the burden of this chapter has been that procedures are of utmost importance in creating a good and fair system of welfare. Good results are achieved only through procedures which are constructed with care and understanding. Procedures also serve the additional function, as we have seen, of ensuring that other important values and principles are upheld and respected. Neglect of these matters will soon lead to criticism and discontent, and to the charge of unfairness. On the other hand, a system which runs according to good and fair procedures will command acceptance and respect. It is difficult to resist the conclusion that the importance of procedures cannot be over-estimated.

4 COMMUNITY CARE: APPLYING PROCEDURAL FAIRNESS

Nick Doyle and Tessa Harding

This chapter explores ways of applying the principles of procedural fairness to the practical provision of welfare services. Community care is taken as the main example, but most of the arguments will apply to other areas of provision.

First we examine the particular features of community care which have a bearing on questions of procedural fairness. We consider how far existing laws help or hinder fair procedures in community care. We then develop proposals for ensuring that fair procedures are established.

Particular features of community care

Here we identify some of the main features of community care which are relevant to discussions of procedural fairness. The list is not exhaustive.

Rights to services?

Legislation on community care relates not to the rights of individuals but to powers or duties for local authorities. Where powers alone exist (as under the National Assistance Act 1948), implementation has been slow and piecemeal. There are always competing priorities for local authority resources, and powers alone cannot ensure that the needs of minorities are addressed. In the 1970s, legislation was introduced which specified duties to provide certain services.[1] In 1986, the Disabled Persons Act imposed a duty to assess the needs of a disabled person for those or other services.[2] The guidance accompanying the NHS and Community Care Act 1990 by contrast, gives local authorities discretion to decide whose needs will be assessed (though they have to publish their criteria for doing so) and indicates that they should provide services 'within available resources'.

There is scope for confusion here, and that discretion is being challenged. The courts and some authorities appear increasingly to accept that where someone has been assessed as needing a service, that service *must* be provided, irrespective of whether or not the authority believes it can afford it.

This has implications for the assessment process. If the outcome of an assessment has enforceable financial consequences, the onus on professional judgement is considerable. It also has profound implications for the rights of disabled people. It is perhaps an indication of how difficult it is to bring such cases, and how little sense of entitlement people have, that there remains a lack of clarity on a matter so crucial to the quality of life of some 12.5 million disabled people and carers.

Procedural fairness

The Disabled Persons Act 1986 conferred certain rights to procedural fairness on disabled people, but some relevant sections of the Act have not been implemented, and the Government has now indicated that they will not be. The following rights have been enacted but not implemented:

* The right to ask for a written statement of the decision resulting from assessment, with reasons for the provision or withholding of services. Local authorities may still choose to do this as a matter of good practice, but it is not a right residing in the individual.

* The right to make their views known at any stage during the assessment process. Instead, the assessor is encouraged, in the White Paper which preceded the NHS and Community Care Act, to consult both parties and take their views into account.

* The right to an appeals procedure, with time limits, and the right to a written response where applicants for community care wish to appeal against decisions about services. The NHS and Community Care Act instead establishes a complaints procedure, intended primarily to address the quality of services provided; it requires complaints to be dealt with by the local authority (which would have made the decisions in the first place); there is no provision for an independent tribunal, nor any procedure for appeals.

* The right of a disabled person to appoint their own authorised representative to present or help present their case, and the right of that representative to have access to information and documents and to attend meetings or interviews concerned with the provision of services. No alternative provisions are proposed.

Local autonomy takes precedence over equity

None of the legislation currently in force confers clear entitlements, nor does it specify what level of services should be available, or what outcomes should be achieved. There is no national consensus about what should be provided, to whom and under what circumstances, or even according to which principles. Under the NHS and Community Care Act, such decisions are to be made locally. Consequently, the distribution of welfare is not in itself fair. There are wide variations in the availability of services between authorities. For example, someone who would qualify for a home help in one area would not in another. The Department of Health publishes figures each year which show wide differences in spending and levels of services per head of population.[3] The principle of autonomy for local decision making has taken precedence over the principles of fairness and equity. Similarly, there is evidence that the distribution of services within authorities is not equitable. For example, people in ethnic minority communities and in rural areas often have more limited access than others with comparable needs.

Unfettered discretion

The passage from the Disabled Persons Act to the NHS and Community Care Act reflects a shift away from procedural rights for people on the receiving end of services, towards additional duties on local authorities. But it is very difficult to ensure that such duties are adequately discharged. Services are in the gift of the local authority and an increasing burden has fallen on professional judgement. As IPPR has argued elsewhere,[4] professionals cannot be expected to police their own decision making satisfactorily. While criteria for decision making are not specified (except where local authorities publish their criteria for assessment), and while service users and applicants have no entitlements, professional discretion is unchecked, unaccountable and open to misuse.

Discriminatory attitudes

People with learning difficulties, mental distress or physical impairments are disadvantaged in a world which fails to cater for them or include them. But these disadvantages are compounded by prejudicial public attitudes and discrimination. They are undervalued and patronised or worse, infantilised. When the costs of community care are estimated, only the direct costs of providing services are taken into account; the financial, social and moral costs of failing to provide services which could enable people to play a full part in society are rarely considered. There is a deeply entrenched and widely held view that disabled people are different, do not have the same aspirations as others, and need to be 'cared for'. Moreover, it is all too common to consider disabled people to be incapable of deciding for themselves and unfit to run their own lives, as passive recipients of the goodwill of others.

Shifting ideologies

Many of the principles of procedural fairness outlined in Galligan's chapter sit uneasily with current concepts of community care. The traditional emphasis on care, compassion and humanity is being challenged from two different quarters. On the one hand, disabled people themselves are demanding a new emphasis on civil rights, equal opportunities and citizenship. They see institutional discrimination as the main disability they face, and are lobbying for new equal rights legislation to outlaw discrimination on grounds of disability.[5] The first priority is equal access to basic essentials such as an adequate income, housing, access to employment, to public transport, to education and to the ordinary facilities of everyday life. Increasingly, the idea of philanthropic services designed and dished out by able-bodied people is also being rejected. Instead, disabled people want to make their own decisions and run their own affairs. This can transform demands for improved local authority services into demands for cash payments, so that they themselves can buy what they need, or for services run by disabled people for disabled people.

On the other hand, the market philosophy of the Conservative Government has stressed efficient targeting of resources and managerial rationality. In the most recent legislation, the NHS and Community Care Act 1990, this philosophy clearly has the upper hand. There is some recognition in this Act of the role of disabled people as *consumers*, who should be consulted about decisions that affect them, who should have certain choices, access to information and a right to complain. But the larger issues of their rights as members of society, or what services, if any, they should be entitled to expect, are not addressed by the Act.

There is some convergence, more apparent than real, between the two positions, in the demands of disabled people to be able to buy what help they choose. But the concept of equal citizenship, which is central to the liberationist philosophy of the disabled people's movement, has no place in the ideology of the marketeers.

Contrast with education

It is instructive to apply the norms of community care to another mainstream welfare service. A local authority has a duty to provide education as well as community care services. If it approached the former as it does the latter, it would have very little idea of how many children of school age lived in the area, and even less how many under-fives or adults might need its services. It would already be providing a certain number of school places. However, it would know that many (but not how many) other children were being educated at home, and that their parents were consequently unable to go out to work. There would be little available to those parents in the way of advice or support, and it would not be clear what educational standards were being achieved. It would, however, be widely accepted that the parents were doing a noble job and saving the local authority a lot of money. There would be periodic scandals about children spending most of the day alone, either at home or on the streets, and receiving no education at all. The local authority would have been told that it must establish the level of educational need in its area and target its resources to those in greatest need. It would be obliged to introduce criteria for allocation, and would establish an assessment process to help teachers decide which children had the greatest educational needs. The limited number of school places would in future be allocated on that basis. By targeting those in greatest need and providing services 'within available resources', the authority would have thus fulfilled its formal requirements.

What community care suffers from above all is a *political failure* to make adequate provision on a fair and equitable basis. Procedural rights are no substitute for adequate policies, but they can address some of the injustices that currently beset community care. They can challenge inequalities, and bring a measure of dignity and respect to individuals. And by these means, they can help to focus public attention on the overriding failure of the political arrangements for community care.

Putting procedural fairness into practice

From the service user's point of view there are three main stages in the relationship with community care providers:
* gaining access to services;
* receiving services;
* review and withdrawal of services.
The challenge is to derive, from the principles outlined by Galligan, procedures which protect individuals' interests throughout each stage.

Gaining access to services

An immutable feature of welfare services is assumed to be that resources can never satisfy the potential demand (although no-one has ever established what that demand might actually be, or how great the shortfall). As a consequence, there is a system of rationing. For the individual, gaining access is about negotiating this system. The following steps are involved:
* finding out about available services;
* applying for services;
* being assessed, to establish eligibility;

* receiving a report on the assessment outcome;
* appealing against assessment outcome – challenging the type or quantity of service offered, or the decision to offer no service.

Receiving services

There should be quality assurance systems linked to the provision of service to successful claimants. For users these systems should take the following forms:
* agreements to be about what services are provided;
* receiving services;
* an accessible means of complaining;

Review and withdrawal of services

This final stage involves the following steps:
* case review;
* appealing against alteration or withdrawal of service;
* exiting from service.

With these stages in mind, we now consider what is required to ensure fairness at each step. We look in detail at:
* information;
* advice, advocacy and representation;
* access;
* promptness;
* handling of individual cases;
* redress through appeals and complaints.

Information for service users

Information is a key to effectiveness and fairness in the system. Without information, people will not know what services are available and whether they might be eligible for them. They will not know how to apply for what they want or how to frame their claim. They will be unable to participate fully in the assessment or review of their case. They will be unable effectively to challenge the outcomes of assessment or review. If their claim is successful, they will not know what standard of service to expect, and thus whether they have grounds for complaint. They will not know about organisations that might help them solve problems in using the service. In short, information is essential if people who are eligible for service are to claim their entitlement.

Although the effects of information deprivation are obvious, the agencies with the principal responsibility for providing welfare support – local authorities – generally perform poorly on telling potential users about their services. Even where information has a high priority, practice usually lags behind aspiration. We would argue that quality of information is an index of an agency's commitment to treating service users with dignity and respect. It is also an index of commitment to some of the other principles referred to – for example, equity. An agency cannot distribute its services equitably if people do not know that they might be eligible to claim them. An equal opportunities policy has little substance if the agency does not make its information accessible to all sections of the community. There is ample evidence, for example, that people in minority ethnic communities and in rural areas are poorly informed about local services and have low expectations of them.

Furthermore, uninformed or ill-informed people are not likely to contribute greatly to the planning of services, nor are they well equipped to act responsibly on their own behalf – by getting involved in the decisions that affect their lives. The supplying of information needs to be proactive, imaginative and participatory, and to take account of the full diversity of people's current experience.

The NHS and Community Care Act has imposed new duties on local authorities to produce community care plans, develop new procedures for assessing needs and managing care services, set up inspection units and other quality assurance systems, and establish complaints procedures. Consultation with service users and with communities is urged, and the Government is encouraging local authorities to produce information about community care services; but this encouragement is in the form of guidance rather than regulation, thus leaving considerable room for discretion. This means that in some authorities information will be more accessible and informative than in others. A few will produce as little information as possible. Many will see following the letter rather than the spirit of guidance as the limit of their obligation to inform.

There are also gaps in the recommendations and suggestions on information. One way of achieving more coherence would be to look at information in relation to the stages listed above. People at each stage have different information needs and, of course, the needs of those who are service users, or applicants for service, are different from those of people who think they may need a service but who have not approached the welfare agency. Different again are the information needs of carers. A satisfactory plan for providing information must take account of these differences. The following problems must be addressed:

* how to grade information so that it is useful in the circumstances in which potential or actual users find themselves;

* how to signpost the route through the levels of detail and guide users to where they want to be;

* how to achieve the appropriate mix of media for conveying the information to the whole population;
* how to inform all potential users;
* how to link the information service to those of other relevant agencies - for example, the education and housing departments of the local authority, the health authority and the family health services authority;
* how to involve service users themselves in the process of defining and meeting information needs.

A well-developed information system should secure the user's entitlement to general information about the welfare agency's role; to detailed information about specific services; and to information about policies, priorities, criteria for eligibility, assessment procedures, what to expect of staff, and redress procedures.

Just as important to service users are rights to all information generated about their particular cases as they move through the system. This general right to be informed should include the following elements:

* the right to a response to communications within a specified time;
* the right to discuss their circumstances with an appropriately qualified person;
* the right to be present on all occasions where their case is discussed;
* the right to copies of all documents relating to their case;
* the right to a written record of significant points arising from any contact with the agency, or of decisions made;
* the right to be consulted about proposals to change procedures or the terms of service;
* the right to be consulted about contacts with other parties about their case;
* the right to be told about sources of independent advice, support, representation or advocacy.

Advice, advocacy and representation

Without advice and the kind of support provided by advice agencies, procedural rights are likely to be a sham for many people. There should, therefore, be a further right to independent advice and, where required, advocacy and/or representation. Fairness can often only be achieved by making life more complicated – through analysing, codifying and elaborating procedural practice. One effect of setting out rights may, therefore, be to make them seem difficult to take up. It is essential that steps are taken to anticipate new demands for advice and support – by working through with advice agencies, including organisations of service users – the advice implications of putting procedural rights into practice.

It can clearly be helpful for an individual facing a particular problem for the first time to have access to people who have been down that road before, who know the ropes and are aware of the options and pitfalls. Such a source of information might be – and often is – another disabled person, or an independent adviser with no axe to grind.

Many of the practical and personal issues on which people require information and advice are crucial to their day-to-day quality of life. They need to know that advisers are impartial and disinterested, and are seeking only to offer expertise, not to exert influence, or to meet objectives of their own. Once people have the information they need, have had the opportunity to consider and discuss it, and have arrived at the right course for them, they may feel equipped to represent their own interests in seeking access to services. But many may not, and would prefer to have a third party acting on their behalf some or all of the time, particularly in the face of a complex world of officialdom, professional language and bureaucratic procedures. For some people, independent representation of their interests by someone who has taken time and trouble to understand their wishes may be essential. It was with this in mind that the Disabled Persons Act established the right of people to appoint their own authorised representatives with powers to act on their behalf – a right which has now been withdrawn, with the non-implementation of this section of the Act.

The difficulty with the current position is that the expected source of relevant information is often the local authority, which is also charged with the rationing of services and has decision-making powers over access to them. The extent to which the authority's advice is independent and disinterested is therefore questionable, since there are likely to be inherent conflicts of interest. It requires independence for an advocacy agency to challenge decisions made on behalf of an individual and to develop an uncompromised overall view of the strengths and weaknesses of local services. Advice and advocacy agencies, whether they be organisations of service users, or independent bodies such as Citizens Advice Bureaux, are better placed than local authorities to fulfil that role – provided, of course, that they themselves have the necessary resources and access to the information required to do the job properly.

Access to the responsible agency

The principle of equity requires that everyone who is eligible to make a claim on a service has the opportunity to do so. It also requires that the agency responsible for community care is organised to ensure that every claim is, as far as possible, appropriately framed and has a fair hearing, as defined by Galligan. We have already argued that information is one of the safeguards of the principle of equity.

However, the right of access can be secured only through the development of good professional and managerial practice. For example, agencies must ensure that front-line staff are trained sufficiently to guide potential users into the system and to help them to apply in the appropriate way. All forms should be in plain language, and there should be versions in the languages of minority communities and in braille. There should be a well-publicised interpreting service. The agency should develop links with local organisations of and for service users.

In addition, the agency should consult service users on performance targets. These targets should be publicised and given to everyone who contacts the agency. Failure to meet any of the targets would be a ground for complaint.

Promptness

In consultation with users, the agency should draw up, publicise and distribute performance targets to ensure promptness at each stage:

* replying to letters and mailing out information and forms requested by phone;
* waiting times at its offices;
* the availability of phone lines and promptness in answering the phone;
* the timetable between application and contact with agency staff responsible for assessing the claim;
* informing users about the progress of their case;
* telling users which agency officers are currently handling their case.

Handling individual cases

All the procedural principles discussed by Galligan in the previous chapter (the hearing principle, giving of reasons, transparency in structuring discretion, impartiality and consistency) must apply directly to the agency's handling of individual cases, particularly at the stages of assessment and review. These principles might be expressed in the following practical ways:

* applicants/users should have a right to all relevant information – as itemised above. In particular, they should be told about organisations and individuals who might be able to advise, counsel or support them; they should be given copies, or be informed, of all facts or other material relevant to their case, including the reports and opinions of other professionals or experts;

* applicants/users should have a right, and must be given the opportunity, to make their own case;
* applicants/users (and, if they choose, a friend, carer or representative) should have a right to be present on all occasions when their case is discussed;
* applicants/users should have a right to a written statement containing the agency's view of their needs; of services required to meet those needs; of the nature and extent of needs which the agency has decided not to meet; and of needs which might be met by another agency;
* applicants/users should have a right to comment on the draft of the statement and to add their comments to the final statement;
* applicants/users should have a right to a written decision, including a statement of reasons for each decision, comprising the facts, the agency's criteria, and an explanation of how the criteria have been applied to the facts;
* applicants/users should have a right to be told how to seek redress.

A fair decision will depend on the impartiality of the agency staff and their commitment to principles of consistency of treatment. Ideally, assessment should result in an objective analysis of needs and a presentation of the options for meeting them *regardless* of cost implications. Thus the agency's decision about which needs it can meet and the services it can provide should not be made by the staff who conducted the assessment. But in practice, even the most conscientious staff are influenced by their knowledge of the agency's priorities and the extent of its resources. They know also that agencies lose credibility or suffer political embarrassment if they too frequently decide not to provide a service, or to provide less than a case objectively merits.

The corruption of the principle of impartiality in these circumstances is well illustrated in the area of educational policy. In theory, parents of children with special educational needs are entitled to an objective diagnosis of those needs and a statement of the provision necessary to meet them. They are also entitled to copies of all the advice sought by the local Education Authority. In practice, statements have been framed in the light of the resources available, and there is good evidence that Education Authorities are putting pressure on those experts whom they are obliged to consult and who are in their employ to suppress advice with cost implications.

The Conservatives argue that splitting the purchaser of services from the provider removes all conflicts of interest. However, the model of care management they recommend in the guidance to the NHS and Community Care Act creates a new conflict. Assessment is supposed to be 'needs-led' yet care managers are to be responsible both for assessment *and* for the budget to buy the service not only for the user in question but also for subsequent function. It might be better if assessments were carried out by a separate agency under contract to the local authority.

Redress through appeals and complaints

The right to seek redress underpins all the other rights we have been discussing. By appealing or complaining, users not only defend their own interests; they also maintain the whole system of welfare rights and associated codes of practice and service guidelines. In addition, effective redress systems also allow users to highlight deficiencies in service and to participate in monitoring standards. There should be two branches to the redress system: one for dealing with complaints; the other for hearing appeals.

Complaints

* The complaints procedure should be for users who are dissatisfied with the service they are receiving, or who think they are receiving less than they are entitled to receive. Users should also be encouraged to complain about indignities inflicted by the agency's staff or contractors, and about failure by the agency to meet its obligations, whether expressed as users' rights, as codes of practice, or as service agreements or performance targets.

* The purpose of the procedure should be to restore the service to the standard previously agreed between user and agency; to ensure that faults are acknowledged; and to provide users with apologies and, if appropriate, compensation.

Only when they know what they are supposed to receive will users be able to gauge service quality, and decide whether they have grounds for complaint. Setting and publicising service standards and putting them in service agreements are important ways of supporting users' rights; they also help the agency by enabling it to monitor its own performance, and thus account better both to its users and to the general public.

Appeals

* The purpose of an appeals mechanism is to give users, or people who want to be users, the opportunity to challenge a decision. In relation to the stages outlined above, people will need the opportunity to appeal when decisions are made following the assessment; when their case is reviewed; and when there is a decision to withdraw a service. In

addition, they will need to be able to appeal if they are dissatisfied with decisions made about their complaints.

* The function of the procedure is to establish whether decisions are fair. This is done by formally reviewing the rigour, first, of the process of assembling information about the user's circumstances, and second, of the practical application to the user's case of the agency's policies.

The NHS and Community Care Act has strengthened the right to complain about welfare services. The guidance that goes with it sets out many of the features that should be in an effective redress system: an emphasis on early resolution; clear, progressive and time-limited stages; and recourse to a hearing before a specially constituted panel at which users can make their case. However, the guidance is almost entirely about enabling current users to complain. It scarcely acknowledges that the people who may have most cause to seek redress are those who have been denied service and want to appeal. Perhaps appellants are higher on the scale of political awkwardness than complainants, in that they expose the rationing system to more scrutiny.

Redress systems are a challenge to the power of the welfare agency; they will not work unless the agency respects users, and treats them with dignity. All the procedural rights so far discussed are designed to shift power toward users so that they have a means not only of gaining their entitlement but also of asserting their worth. As agencies are most formidable when challenged, users need the guarantee of support when seeking redress. Support should be available in two main forms: advocacy and independent review. As we have argued above, access to independent advocacy is essential: advocacy services must be developed, coordinated and properly funded.

Independent review

Users who are dissatisfied with the agency's handling of their complaint or appeal should have recourse to an independent, local, investigative body. Ideally, this would be a local version of the Commission for Local Administration (the Local Ombudsman) with a similar brief – that is, to investigate complaints arising from maladministration, and to secure redress for the complainant. (The Commission itself would, of course, remain as a last resort.) It might be that such a scheme would work best if it covered all of an authority's services, not just welfare services. A broad remit would tend to increase the ombudsman's independence from any one department – and without any loss of expertise, since the principles of good procedural practice apply regardless of the service provided. There might even be scope for neighbouring authorities jointly to establish a shared ombudsman scheme.

Another form of independent review is discussed in relation to health care in Chapter 5: the patient's right to a second opinion. Since many appeals in community care are not about maladministration (the province of the Ombudsman) but about the exercise of professional judgement, there is a case for making available to potential service users and carers a right to a second opinion from a suitably qualified independent practitioner. Such a right could help to ensure that appropriate expertise is brought to bear on the circumstances of individuals in relation to their particular needs – for example, their cultural background or specific impairment.

Conclusion

It is important for the agencies responsible for making decisions about people's access to services to take to heart the concept of procedural rights, and to ensure that such rights are enshrined in their own policy and practice. This in itself will require substantial changes, not least in attitudes.

Nonetheless, it would be dangerous to leave responsibility for such rights exclusively in the hands of those who already exercise power over the day-to-day lives of individuals. Effective independent representation is needed to safeguard the rights of individuals, and to help ensure that they become more widely acknowledged. For procedural rights to exist in reality rather than just on paper, they have to be capable of being exercised by the individual concerned, whether that individual is eventually judged right or wrong in their claim, and irrespective of the practice of the agency concerned. Galligan points out that the right to be heard is the first principle of natural justice. Yet in the field of community care, rights to be heard, to be represented if so desired, and to put one's case to an independent arbitrator, have yet to be established.

5 RIGHTS TO HEALTH AND HEALTH CARE

Jonathan Montgomery

This chapter considers the role of welfare rights in health. At one level it is an exercise in social policy, seeking to set out and justify a blueprint for promoting health and protecting patients' rights. At another, it examines the difficulties and possibilities of implementing this social policy through a legal framework. It is easy to establish a persuasive rhetoric of rights, but this can be rendered meaningless if rights are not put into practice. A successful scheme of health rights requires a strategic blend of rights and duties. This chapter not only looks at what might be the content of health rights, but also considers a strategy for implementation.

Health rights have a long-established place in international rights documents, and it would be difficult to argue against the importance of good health. Nevertheless, introducing the concept of a right to health raises a number of problems. This chapter concentrates on two of the most important. First, health rights cannot exist without imposing duties to respect or promote health. To say that someone has a right usually implies that someone else has an obligation in respect of that right.[1] There is room for disagreement about exactly who should be placed under such obligations and about their precise content; but unless some sort of duty exists, the claims being made are not rights, but have a lesser status. The claim being made here for legal health rights implies that these duties should be legally enforceable, and not remain as moral aspirations. This means identifying the organisations and persons on which obligations should be imposed. It is also necessary to spell out the ways in which these obligations are enforced.

Second, to argue that a person has a right to make a claim upon the state implies that this claim must be given some sort of priority.[2] Rights need not be absolute in the sense that they must always prevail over other policy considerations; but establishing individual rights is a way of giving greater weight to certain claims of individuals over collective interests. This is a valuable aspect of the idea of rights, but it also makes it necessary to guard against their inappropriate use. Rights constrain the democratic process in order to protect minorities against the 'tyranny of the majority'. Yet an excessive and inappropriate use of rights might actually block social reform. Thus a libertarian rights-based vision can reduce the powers of the state to a such a level that welfare provision becomes unconstitutional and a violation of individual rights.[3] To sum up, it is not enough to argue that health is so important that health rights must be created; it is vital to determine what manner of rights they should be.

This chapter begins with an examination of the place of health rights within a framework of citizens' rights in a modern welfare system. It first considers the principles to be followed, and then looks at the problems of implementing health rights. The abstract expression of health rights needs to be supplemented by a framework of more specific legal duties. Some of these duties can be aimed at achieving particular outcomes, but others must be concerned with the way in which decisions about health are made, challenged, or carried out.

A new Rights of Patients Act is proposed, which would establish certain specific and enforceable rights. It would also set up a new complaints procedure, and bring other legislation into line. It would oblige the Secretary of State to provide, by statutory instrument, a Code of Patients' Rights which embodies ideals of good practice in the delivery of health care: the rights in the Code would not be enforceable, but breaches of the Code would be grounds for complaint under the new procedure; they could also be taken into account by the courts and bodies concerned with professional discipline. A comparison of this Code with the Conservative Government's Patient's Charter' highlights the importance of the framework of enforcement. Application of the Patients' Rights Act would not be restricted to the public sector: all patients, whether public or private, should have equal rights. At present, controls on private health care are minimal. Under the proposed scheme, patients would be entitled to use the courts whatever the source of their treatment or care.

The complexity of the UK health-care system requires a variety of techniques to ensure enforcement of health rights. Currently, both the principles to which patients can appeal and the mechanisms through which they can act are haphazard and confusing. The network of legal duties and mechanisms for enforcement proposed here is based on a uniform set of principles, but recognises that not all can be enforced in the same way and that not all means of enforcement can be effective in all circumstances.

The idea of health rights

Health is a pre-requisite for individuals to participate fully in the life of society.[4] Without it, choices are seriously curtailed. People who are physically and mentally ill may not be deliberately prevented from acting as they wish, but they may still be unable to do so. Fundamental rights which aim to allow people to make their own choices would clearly need to include a commitment to health. Utilitarian arguments could point to the role of good health in promoting personal happiness or economic productivity, while egalitarians could show that social inequality is linked with inequity of health. Which ever way you look at it, preserving and restoring the health of citizens is a fundamental task of a responsible state.

If civil rights are to be of any value, citizens must be able to exercise them, and ill-health provides a major obstacle to this. Like rights to life and liberty, the right to health is one of the group of basic rights which makes active citizenship possible. As Raymond Plant argues, fundamental freedoms such as democratic participation and expression are at risk unless the citizen is protected from the causes of ill-health and provided with health services.

If health rights are to mean anything, the state must support their enforcement. The same is true of all basic rights, even those of forbearance, or negative' rights, such as personal security. These rights are sometimes said to require only that individual citizens refrain from acting in ways which harm others. It is argued that they cost nothing, and make no claim on scarce resources. It is also suggested that only such costless claims can properly be described as fundamental human rights, because they are the only type of claim which can be guaranteed full recognition. If true, this would challenge the case for health rights. But this argument is fatally flawed, as Raymond Plant demonstrates. Even negative rights are ineffective without protective state agencies such as a police force and a criminal justice system. Without such costly enforcement measures there would be no rights' at all, because the very concept of a right implies some form of sanction. The debate is, in fact, not over whether steps should be taken by the state to protect rights, but what steps are needed and how to implement them.

The United Kingdom is already committed by a number of international agreements to promote health rights. The Universal Declaration of Human Rights states that:

> Everyone has the right to a standard of living adequate for the health
> and well-being of himself and his family, including food, clothing,
> housing and medical care and necessary social services. . . . (Article 25)

This is further expressed in Article 12 of the International Covenant on Economic, Social and Cultural Rights as:

> the right to enjoyment of the highest attainable standard of physical
> and mental health.

A more detailed exposition is set out in the European Social Charter. As a signatory, the United Kingdom is bound to take steps to guarantee safe conditions of work (Article 3), to remove the causes of ill-health, to promote health education, to eradicate disease (Article 11) and to ensure the provision of necessary health care for those without the resources to secure it (Article 13).

If such commitments are to be put into practice, the aspirations of general health rights must be translated into specific legal rules. These must impose obligations on identifiable people or authorities, and provide remedies to ensure that they are carried out. Otherwise, there is no guarantee that health rights will be taken seriously.[5] However, not all legitimate steps taken in the interests of public health can or should be turned into enforceable legal rights. Rights should be created where the interests of individual citizens justify imposing obligations on other people or organisations. Some issues, such as controlling the consumption of alcohol, are not clear cut. While intervention may be desirable, it is not certain that it is *necessary*, or that health concerns outweigh other considerations. It is a matter for democratic debate. Citizens need both to retain rights to concern and respect for their health and to participate in the decision-making process. A flexible framework is needed to guarantee that both sets of rights are recognised.

Rights must also be designed to foster a democratic society. Health rights could be realised by imposing general obligations, and relying on the government or official agencies to police them. However, a commitment to empower citizens and patients demands more than this. The legal rules must make the decision-makers, so far as is possible, responsive to the needs and priorities of individual citizens. Without this second objective, legal authority to pursue public health may serve the interests of the professionals more than individuals. It may enable professionals to impose their ideas of health on citizens. And, as IPPR has argued elsewhere, professionals do not always know best.[6]

One of the weaknesses of the reforms introduced by the National Health Service and Community Care Act 1990 is the way in which they treat the devolution of power to general practitioners as equivalent to increased patient choice.[7] The White Paper, *Working for Patients*, was committed to giving patients greater choice. The Act seeks to achieve this by delegating decision-making to local levels, but does nothing to take it out of the hands of professionals. The new 'internal market' is one in which both purchasers and suppliers are health service personnel. New fund-holding general practices are able to exercise choices in the health market place, but are likely to reflect what doctors believe is in the interests of their practice. It is assumed that this is also in the interests of patients, but the only sanction available to dissatisfied patients is to leave the practice and take their capitation fee elsewhere.

The health rights proposed here are intended to secure respect for claims made by individuals in the support of their health, not to entrench the power of health professionals to speak on behalf of their patients.

International documents about rights remain highly abstract. Before a detailed programme for the implementation of health rights can be drawn up, three issues must be tackled. First, there are conceptual difficulties: what, for example, is 'health' and what causes ill-health? We must consider the former to establish the content of health rights, and the latter to identify appropriate strategies to deal with them. Second, we need an assessment of the types of rights and duties which might be available. Individual entitlements claimed directly from the relevant agencies will be suitable for some areas. In others, collective or group rights of some sort will be more effective. Third, the dangers of an excessively coercive use of the idea of health rights need to be discussed.

'Health' and the causes of ill-health

Before elaborating the scope of health rights, it is important to establish whether the objective of health rights is to maximise the health of citizens, or merely to maintain a minimal level of health adequate for work and leisure. The constitution of the World Health Organisation refers to health as 'a state of complete physical, mental and social well-being and not merely the absence of disease.'[8] This is a maximal concept, in that it aspires to the highest possible standard and sees health' as a target which is rarely fully attained, although worthy of pursuit. Others look no further than the absence of ill-health, defining an average standard of well-being as 'healthy' and allowing for an excess of well-being as well as a deficit. Clearly, health rights based on the former approach will be more extensive than those grounded in the latter.

Concepts of health also depend on social and historical conditions. Homosexuality, for example, was once classified as an illness. Now, it would be an unacceptable concept of health rights to force homosexuals to change their sexual orientation in the name of good health. Similarly, even when prevailing fashion regards fat as unhealthy, it is surely legitimate for people to decide for themselves to be fat rather than thin. And the history of mental health shows that definitions of sanity and insanity are constantly shifting.

Good health cannot (and should not) be forced upon citizens. Any system of health rights must protect individuals against being forced to conform in a way which may unnecessarily compromise their freedom. Policy makers rely on experts who claim objective knowledge, and in this way the role of ordinary citizens in defining health needs gets ignored.[9] Overzealous health promotion may also deny individuality to those with unusual health requirements, or to those who regard ill-health as an acceptable cost of other benefits they might pursue. Banning all tobacco products, for example, would prevent people from choosing to balance the health risks against the pleasures of smoking. It is therefore necessary to ensure public accountability in health promotion programmes. Setting them in an inflexible legal framework could become repressive.

These problems present difficulties in any attempt to specify health rights and their limitations. It is pointless to try to define the precise content of a maximal concept of 'health': further improvements will always be possible. It is less readily conceded that a minimal standard is subject to similar ambiguity. Some argue that objectivity is possible by reference to biological norms.[10] They present the idea of 'normal species functioning' as a biological fact rather than a social construct. Yet what is accepted as normal is itself a social judgement. This can perhaps be seen most clearly in relation to the effects of age. It is usual for the human body to become less powerful as it grows older, but the degree to which debilitation is acceptable (and therefore left untreated) is a matter for social judgement. We no longer accept impaired mobility for the elderly as a matter of course. Hip replacements, for example, are now both routine and desirable; before, it might have been thought normal to become immobilised. Whether based upon a minimal or maximal standard, the content of health rights will depend on what is currently technically possible and appropriate to the social context. In that case, to enshrine standards too specifically in the law may prove restrictive, blocking advances in technology or expectations.

From this perspective, it could be argued that these problems can only be overcome by limiting health rights to those maintaining minimum standards. In terms of the philosophical basis for rights, this is because only an adequate state of health is necessary for citizens to function. Being healthy is a precondition of citizenship, but being in excellent health is not. In this view, while promoting the best possible standards is a proper task for government is it is not a matter of citizens' rights. A maximal state of good health is good for people and it is good for the economy, but the degree to which the state pursues it without infringing fundamental rights is a matter of debate. Thus, the proper place to establish the limits of health promotion is within the normal democratic processes.

Nevertheless, a case can be made for rights to health which are not limited to minimal standards. It rests first on the acknowledged benefits of prevention rather than cure. Measures which prevent ill-health maintain basic health, and must be pursued in order to ensure a minimum standard of health for all, even if this means making some already healthy people even more healthy. People's health needs are interdependent. In practice, it is not possible to stop at the basic level because it means that some people may not reach even that level. The only way to be sure of attaining even the lowest level of health is to aim high.

In addition, the threshold of minimal acceptable health is likely to be raised as the structural causes of ill-health are tackled. A lower standard will always be left behind and become unsatisfactory. Finally, the more a society seeks to promote full participation by its citizens, the greater the scope for health rights. Better health permits fuller choice and involvement in public life. The suggestion that maximal rights are not justified because only minimal health is required for civic activity assumes that needs are constant. In fact, our understanding of what citizenship implies is also developing constantly. A minimalist approach to health rights must not be allowed to act as a brake on this kind of progress.

To these arguments against adopting a limited view of the concept of health can be added the complex causes of ill-health. While some types of illness, most clearly those connected with specific diseases, can be traced back to particular sources, this is not always the case. Historically, significant advances in public health have been achieved through improvements in sanitation, diet, housing and the environment rather than medical intervention.[11] In addition, it has consistently been shown that there is a correlation between general social and economic disadvantage and ill-health.[12] These causes of ill-health cannot be overcome simply by the provision of health services. A much broader approach is needed to minimise social and economic inequality, reduce poverty and mitigate its impact on the health of individuals.

It would seem, in conclusion, that a maximal concept of health is appropriate in the context of aspirational health rights, such as those which might be enshrined in a social charter. But when it comes to enforceable rights, a maximal concept may be inappropriate. What we need is a combination of approaches: individually enforceable rights to safeguard minimal standards; aspirational rights to direct policy and practice towards the continuous improvement of the nation's health, and legal obligations to secure the conditions that make it possible for citizens to choose to pursue maximal health. This last approach requires some sort of group rights.

Group rights

Progress relating to the wider influences on people's health can be achieved only by collective action. An adequate framework of health rights will therefore need to provide for collective as well as individual rights. Two categories of group rights are important here. The first provides for action by a group on behalf of its individual members. Thus patients' rights organisations could raise complaints on behalf of those they represent. Such group rights are a means of protecting the interests of citizens where individual enforcement would be ineffective. For example, a representative body could take up a complaint about persistent disregard for patients' rights, whereas an individual complaint would not be considered serious enough to warrant the time and effort.

In some cases this will not be enough and a second type of group right is called for, which recognises that intermediate agencies are needed to monitor and enforce standards. This may be because citizens have to challenge powerful vested interests. For example, in the context of health and safety at work, employees as individuals may be vulnerable to pressure to conform with employers' demands. An independent agency could act more effectively on their behalf. This is one of the principles behind freedom of association and the trade union movement.

Agencies may also be needed with powers to investigate and enforce which could not be given to an individual. The control of pollution, for example, cannot be left to individuals because environmental damage is suffered collectively. Unless 'special damage' has occurred no individual will have a right to sue. An enforcement agency, however, can bring an action in the public interest. There is a risk that it might take power away from citizens, but where individuals cannot be directly empowered it is better to recognise their rights indirectly through collective action than to leave them without legal force. Organisations can play an important role in ensuring that the preconditions for good health are maintained. Such bodies already operate (with varying degrees of effectiveness) in relation to health and safety at work, food safety, environmental health and control of pollution.

A right to be unhealthy?

Accepting the importance of a wide-ranging right to health increases the risk that people may be forced to be healthy against their will. This is particularly difficult in relation to collective action to improve the environments in which people live and work. If, for example, one person chooses to drink unclean water where there is a risk of a cholera epidemic, the rights of that individual cannot be allowed to outweigh those of the majority. But a more delicate balancing exercise may be needed for a health promotion strategy such as the fluoridation of water. Only the young benefit from fluoridation while some evidence suggests that excess fluoride may be harmful. If a right to fluoridated water were held to be part of the fundamental right to health, debate about how these considerations should be balanced would be precluded. Such matters should be on the agenda for public consideration and not predetermined by constitutional rights.

A particular problem arises with those with contagious diseases, including HIV. Existing law balances the rights of those who are ill with those of the general public by providing powers to quarantine but not to administer compulsory treatment. Some of these powers are now extended to people with HIV. Yet the legislation assumes that the disease is highly infectious and curable – and HIV is neither. Thus, the effect of the extension of the public health measures infringes the civil liberties of those with or suspected of carrying the virus.[13] The law permits magistrates to make orders for compulsory testing and detention without allowing sufferers to put their case. While this may be appropriate for infections which must be controlled rapidly if there is to be any chance of successful containment, it is unnecessary in the case of a virus which is as difficult to transmit as HIV. This illustrates the dangers of prescribing the details of public health law in general terms. Each public health problem needs its own appropriate framework.

Socially acceptable practices with significant health implications raise further difficulties. Much ill-health can be traced to traffic accidents, diet, the use of alcohol and tobacco. However, it would be wrong to seek to eradicate these threats to health, whether for strictly practical reasons (as with road transport), or because they help people cope with stress (as with the use of stimulants), or because they represent the exercise of the very freedom which civil rights are supposed to protect. Nevertheless, health rights demand that citizens are protected from ill effects so far as is compatible with their (and others') right to shape their own lifestyle. In order to make informed choices, citizens must be entitled to relevant information; controls on advertising may be needed to stop manufacturers hiding health risks.

Under these principles, health can be promoted through measures which define the manner of such activities, but do not prohibit them. Prescribing the wearing of seat-belts comes into this category. It is important, however, to avoid limiting the manner of an activity to such an extent that doing it ceases to be practicable. For example, banning smoking on public transport is legitimate while it is permitted in other public places. A ban on selling alcohol which prevents access by a whole community would be unacceptable. In certain cases, even limited restrictions may infringe important freedoms. For example, to protect their religious freedom, Sikhs are not forced to wear motor-cycle helmets although non-Sikhs are.

Implementing health rights

An effective framework for health rights requires a co-ordinated network of rights and obligations at a number of levels. If there is to be a 'Social Charter' for Britain, as Lewis and Seniveratne propose, a right to health would of course be enshrined in it. Such a Charter would be a means to ensure that all government policy had to take account of the impact on citizens' health.

The precise wording of health rights in a social charter remains a matter of debate. Norman Lewis has proposed one form of words, based on the European Social Charter and the European Code of Social Security. An alternative draft article is set out below. Much of its content is taken from the European Social Charter. Unlike the European Social Charter, however, the detailed provisions are framed not in terms of the obligations of the government, but of the rights of every citizen. This emphasises the grounding of government duties in the interests of individuals. A balance is struck between government and individual responsibility. There is a right to the preconditions of good health, an adequate standard of living (Clause 1) and the absence of threats to health (Clauses 2 to 4). These deal with areas which cannot be achieved through personal choice alone. Clause 5 recognises that a programme of health promotion cannot be forced on unwilling individuals: citizens must be provided with information but be free to decide how they use it. Clause 6 is concerned with health care.

Draft article for the Charter of Welfare Rights

Everyone has a right to the highest attainable standard of health, including:
(1) A right to a standard of living adequate for their good health and that of their family.
(2) A right to safe working conditions.
(3) A right that the government work to remove the causes of ill-health.
(4) A right to government measures to prevent and control the existence and spread of disease.
(5) A right to information enabling them to take responsibility for protecting, maintaining and improving their health and that of their family.
(6) A right to health care appropriate to their needs.
A British Social Charter by itself would not be enough. In order to guarantee that specific tasks are carried out, identifiable authorities would need to be given responsibility, and appropriate enforcement mechanisms provided.

English law already recognises that the implementation of a right to safe working conditions requires:

 * duties on employers to provide a safe work place, with rights of
 employees to receive compensation for injuries caused in breach of these
 duties;

 * government agencies to advise on dangers and how they should be
 overcome, backed up by regulations imposing criminal penalties for
 failure to meet the required standards;

 * an inspectorate with power to enter the workplace, to issue formal
 warnings, close premises and prosecute.

These existing provisions fail to ensure employee participation, for which further rights would be necessary. On the positive side, however, they meet the need for concrete detail in safeguarding health (for example, the possible causes of injury and ways to avoid them). They also illustrate the principle that intermediate bodies are required to make health rights effective.

Specific agencies of this sort currently oversee health and safety at work, food safety and environmental health, each under its own statute. In addition, an independent body, funded by central government, is needed to co-ordinate health education and research. This body would be responsible for enabling citizens to take responsibility for the health implications of their lifestyles. Citizens could obtain information from it on public health issues. It would also identify areas for research on public health. The nearest we have to such a body at present is the Health Education Authority (formerly the Health Education Council): this comes under the auspices of the NHS, and has proved to be vulnerable to political interference. The IPPR has elsewhere endorsed proposals for a Public Health Commission,[14] which would, in addition to other functions, serve as a stronger alternative to the HEA.

Rights to health care

The idea that there should be a right to appropriate health care (set out in Clause 6 of the proposed Charter) raises a problem so far left untouched – how to make health rights enforceable by the citizens in whose interests they are created. It is not always practicable for individuals to police obligations directly. First, enforceability requires rights to be defined in a clear manner. This is difficult where there is uncertainty about the causes and cures for ill-health. Health rights which are defined in terms of outcomes – a right to specific health status – would be unworkable, because they may be impossible to achieve given available knowledge. For example, the right to conceive a child: some causes of infertility can be overcome, but others cannot. A right which could not be satisfied would undermine the very idea of health rights and reduce them to empty rhetoric.

One possibility would be to define the right in terms of access to all available treatment. Here, however, the scarcity of resources produces difficulties. Although the state can properly be required to commit resources to health promotion and care, individually enforceable rights might constrain legitimate planning about how these resources are allocated. The numbers of kidneys available for transplant or dialysis machines will always be limited. They are only useful when given to specific patients who need them. A system of allocation is therefore vital. It may be the right of potential recipients that steps be taken to ensure an adequate supply and to be treated fairly on decisions about allocation, but not all patients can have a meaningful right to receive a kidney when there are not enough to go around. The best that can be managed in terms of individually enforceable rights is probably a right to be considered for treatment, a right to reasons when denied it, and an opportunity to challenge discriminatory or otherwise unreasonable decisions. (The general principles of procedural fairness are explored in Chapter 2. In the end, however, the problem of scarcity makes managerial discretion inevitable. It is necessary to look for types of rights which are compatible with this discretion but which make its exercise accountable.

It is also important to protect the interests of citizens who are unlikely to benefit from the introduction of enforceable rights, and may even lose out through it. Some health needs do not lend themselves to being cast as individual entitlements. While it may be possible to specify a right to a specific treatment like dialysis, doing so might force the diversion of resources from other projects which are not required by right.[15] Hospital building and refurbishment programmes would be particularly vulnerable, because they can rarely be linked directly to the needs of identifiable individuals in a compelling way. Even if enforceable rights are created, they will be used unevenly, and organised groups are likely to benefit far more than those individuals who do not press their claims. In particular, the interests of people who are elderly and/or mentally incapacitated would need to be protected.

As well as the problem of limited resources, there is the question of the decisions surrounding treatment and rates of success. These are technical judgements not easily made by lay people. The advice of health professionals is an integral part of the process of selecting appropriate treatment. This affects not only the choices made in particular cases, but also the practicality of specifying health rights. The European Social Charter refers to 'the care necessitated by his [the individual's] condition'. Determining what is necessary will mean importing professional advice. Thus, in addition to managerial issues, there will also be an element of professional discretion involved in the implementation of health-care rights. That is not to say, however, that all aspects of professional decision-making should be beyond public scrutiny.

If we accept that there is a place for managerial and professional discretion, this affects the way in which health rights are defined and enforced. Rights expressed in terms of outcomes must be qualified – for example, a right to treatment would become a right to 'appropriate' and 'available' treatment. But it is important to establish that the way in which such qualifications are determined should also be the subject of health rights. Citizens should be given the right to informed participation in decisions and the right to challenge the results. This is as true of the relationship between patients and professionals as of the wider debate on resource allocation. Maximising public and patient involvement requires an integrated web of rights and duties.

A Rights of Patients Act

The position of individual patients receiving care should be strengthened by a range of new measures. Our proposal is for a new Rights of Patients Act, providing a limited number of enforceable legal rights for individual patients. The Act would provide for a Code of Patients Rights' which would set standards for good practice in service delivery: this would not be directly enforceable, but could be taken into account in legal and complaints proceedings.

Enforceable rights would cover consent, confidentiality, and access to records: matters which define the patient's relationship with the professional. In addition, a right to seek a second opinion should be created, for which responsibility would lie with the relevant family health service authority (FHSA) or (in the case of hospital care) district health authority (DHA). The Act would also seek to ensure access to health care on a fair and equitable basis, and the right of patients to a written treatment plan. Where necessary, it would amend existing legislation. The new statutory rights would be enforceable through a complaints procedure set up under the Act, and through the courts.

The following section considers in detail the content of the Rights of Patients Act, including the Code. We look first at how the new Act would affect other legislation, particularly in relation to access to health care. We then deal in some detail with the proposed rights to consent, confidentiality and access to records. Next, we examine the functions of the Code of Patients' Rights. In the final section we consider three aspects of enforcement: a new complaints procedure, professional discipline and compensation.

Access to health care

Overall responsibility for providing health services must remain the statutory obligation of the Secretary of State for Health, under the National Health Service Act 1977. Existing law does not provide for an enforceable right to treatment, although an unreasonable refusal or the withholding of treatment for improper reasons may be subject to judicial review. Since the level of public resources committed to health is a matter for political debate, it is not appropriate to establish the exact level of provision by law. It is, however, possible to move towards greater public participation in decision-making. The Act should lay specific obligations upon the Secretary of State for Health and on the health authorities to consult the public before taking decisions about the allocation of resources, and to make their decisions available to the public. This would make decisions more readily accountable through parliamentary channels, and facilitate judicial review on the limited basis of the courts' jurisdiction.

In some cases, access to health care is prevented by the decisions of individual doctors. The right to change your GP is an important factor in overcoming such restrictions. This right has recently been strengthened, and its effectiveness should continue to be monitored. GPs who exercise their right to refuse patients or to remove them from their lists should be required by the Act to provide written reasons, and citizens would be entitled to challenge them under the new complaints procedure.

Where professionals exercise statutory rights of conscience (regarding abortion and some types of infertility treatment), they should be required to inform patients that they are doing so and refer them to a person who is prepared to provide that care. This is not clear under the existing provisions. The Act should amend the Abortion Act 1967 (Section 4) and the Human Fertilisation and Embryology Act 1990 (Section 38) to this effect.

The Act would also give patients a right to a written treatment plan in which the assessment, proposed treatment and reasonable alternatives were recorded. This might be no more than a copy of the relevant notes. An obligation to provide written information is already in place for opticians and dentists. Patients could complain about failures to keep to the agreed plans, or about plans being misleading. Those who suffer minor financial loss as a result of culpable failures to honour promises could gain compensation through the complaints procedure. More substantial sums of money could be pursued through the courts. (See below, p.106, for more on compensation.)

The speed with which health services respond to patients' needs could also be addressed by the Act. GPs and specialists would be required to assess patients' needs and relevant health authorities would be required to make treatment available – all within a mutually agreed time. This agreement could be enshrined in a form of contract. The time periods for assessment and treatment would not be set down by the law, but standards would be set in the Code of Patients' Rights, and the Act itself would require FHSAs and DHAs to publish targets. Failure to meet them would allow for a grievance to be brought within the complaints procedure.

Consent

At present, English law does not recognise the doctrine of informed consent. It says there must be 'real' consent before treatment is lawful. However, the amount of information required to make it 'real' is minimal. Complaints about the level of information provided are treated as general issues of malpractice in the same way as errors of diagnosis and care: patients must establish that they have suffered as a result of professional negligence. This means that cases turn on prevailing professional standards, and if there is a responsible body of professional opinion prepared to support what has been done, it is very difficult for a patient to win a case. Judges have often indicated their belief that information should be given to patients in order to make their consent fully informed, but they have refused to enforce this through the law.

The Act should make it clear that a failure to provide the patient with all the information a prudent person would want would constitute a *prima facie* case of negligence. Health professionals would be permitted to answer such a case by showing that the patient had expressly declined to exercise their right to receive the information, or that the professional had compelling reasons for believing that disclosure would cause serious harm to the patient's health. In assessing both what a reasonably prudent patient would require and what would constitute serious harm, the court would be directed to the Code of Patients' Rights (although departure from the Code would not necessarily be considered negligent). Where a doctor knew or ought to have known that the particular patient wanted more information than would normally be required, then a failure to reveal the additional information would also raise a *prima facie* case of malpractice.

Existing law makes it clear that in principle a competent patient is entitled to refuse treatment recommended by the responsible health professionals. The Act should make it clear, in line with past judicial comments, that this can be for any reason or no reason.

The Act should also provide – but in this case through the Code, rather than as a statutory duty – that professionals should take into account advance declarations as to refusals of care or the wishes of proxies appointed by patients to take decisions on their behalf. Advance directives, or living wills, are documents in which a person states their wishes as to future treatment, including perhaps being allowed to die. Under existing law there is no clear obligation to respect such wishes, so that by declaring patients incompetent, professionals can override their desire to be left to die.

Giving full legal effect to advance refusals is likely to be counter-productive. The drastic impact on the position of both patient and professional and the dangers of abuse would make the courts interpret the terms of the documents narrowly and quite possibly contrary to the patient's intentions.[16] Placing the provisions on living wills in the Code rather than as a statutory right in the Act would give rise to fewer problems. The Code should include the right to make a living will, and state that such wills should normally be followed by professionals. If a living will were ignored then a complaint could be made, and in assessing it the investigating officer or professional body concerned would consider why the Code had been breached.

The new law on consent also needs to protect the interests of patients who are unable to give valid consents. These include some young children and people who are mentally incapacitated (whether by disability, illness or senility). Detailed provisions have already been made for mentally disordered people by the Mental Health Act 1983 and the Code of Practice made under it. The scope of parental consent to the treatment of children should be made explicit within the sections of the Act. It is already clear that this does not extend to permitting sterilisations, which must be approved by a court. A similar limitation should be imposed in relation to the donation of organs and withholding of life-saving treatment. The Act should also make it clear that competent children have as much right to refuse treatment as to consent to it.[17] (Priscilla Alderson considers the questions of children's competence and consent in more detail in Chapter 8.)

The general position in relation to mentally incapacitated adults is governed by a decision of the House of Lords which allows professionals to do whatever they think is in the best interests of an incompetent patient. This is unsatisfactory in that it leaves decisions entirely to the health professions, without any effective mechanism for review. The Act should specify that approval by an independent assessor is required before irreversible measures are taken, in the same way that parental consent is limited in relation to children.

Confidentiality

A statutory right of confidentiality needs to be introduced in order to safeguard the rights of patients to privacy. The legal force of such a right is at present uncertain. So far as it does exist, the courts have held that it is based on the public interest in the efficiency of health care and not on the individual rights of patients. This needs to be changed, so that all information about a patient gathered by health professionals, from whatever source, is confidential (subject to strictly limited exceptions).

These exceptions would be, first, by the consent of the patient (or their representative in the case of incompetent patients). There would be a general presumption that patients consented to information being shared with other health professionals in the course of care, although individual patients would be entitled to veto such sharing. Second, patient confidentiality could be breached if it were in the public interest to do so, but only where there is a serious risk of danger to an identifiable individual, and only to the extent necessary to enable the reduction of risk. Disclosure of information to the patient's family would not be permitted unless it were the only way to prevent serious (and likely) damage to the health of one of its members. Apart from the specific exceptions, confidential information would be released only in accordance with a statutory obligation or in court proceedings when required by a judge. These exceptions are broadly in line with those accepted by the nursing professional body, but are more restrictive than those currently recognised by the General Medical Council.

Patients would be entitled to injunctions restraining a breach of confidentiality, and to financial compensation if such a breach occurred and consequently cost them money. An obligation of confidence would also be part of the Code of Patients' Rights. Breaches of confidence could therefore be the subject of complaints and professional disciplinary proceedings even where no damage occurred that was quantifiable in money terms.

Access to health records

Rights to see your own health records are a vital part of a framework of health rights. Access to the records enables patients to correct inaccurate information and to learn more about their condition. Rights already exist under the Data Protection Act 1984 (in relation to computerised records) and the Access to Health Care Records Act 1990 (with effect from November 1991). The provisions of the 1990 Act should be consolidated into the Rights of Patients Act and extended to computerised records so that a single framework exists. This would prevent confusion when the wrong procedure is used, and make all the provisions guaranteeing patients' rights available in a single place. No changes of substance are proposed, but the procedure should be streamlined so that avenues for complaint are uniform for all aspects of health care. It should be made clear by the Act that complaints can be brought if the health professionals use their discretion to deny access in the name of the patient's interests, and that the investigating officer would be entitled to see all the records in order to judge whether the refusal of access was justified.

The Code of Patients' Rights

The Code of Patients' Rights would be set up by statutory instrument under the Rights of Patients Act, following consultation with interested bodies, including those representing service users. To prevent delay, there should be an obligation laid down in the Act to publish the Code within twelve months of the Act coming into force. Changes could be made by further statutory instrument when necessary.

A number of examples of such codes already exist. The earliest and most familiar is the Highway Code. The most important precedent in this case is the Code of Practice issued under the Mental Health Act 1983, which gives detailed guidance on proper standards of care. A code of practice has also been drawn up by the Human Fertilisation and Embryology Authority to govern embryo research and certain types of fertility treatment. Here the main sanction supporting the code is the fact that it will be taken into account when the renewal of licences is considered. The Code of Patients' Rights would have a similar status in relation to nursing homes, where the extent to which its requirements are met would be a factor in allowing continued registration.

Like the Highway Code and the Mental Health Act Code of Practice, the Code of Patients' Rights can offer detailed guidance as to what is appropriate, rather than a series of heavy-handed statutory prohibitions; it can enshrine standards to which society aspires as well as minimum acceptable standards.

The first function of the Code would be to enable patients to know what they are entitled to expect from their health professionals. It would also ensure that health professionals know where they stand.

The Code of Patients' Rights would not itself have the force of law. The goal is for health care to be delivered to all patients according to the standards set out in the Code, but this calls for a high degree of detail, and it would be counter-productive to make every failure to meet the standards a breach of the law. It would encourage a restrictive and legalistic approach to interpretation and be unacceptable to the healthcare professions. Nevertheless, it would be taken into account by employers and by the various professional bodies in disciplinary proceedings, as well as by the local investigators and the Health Service Commissioners in relation to complaints, and by the courts in mal-practice actions. The Act should establish that a failure to abide by the Code of Patients' Rights would be *prima facie* evidence that a professional had acted negligently or improperly. They would be required to justify the departure, and if they could not explain it then the court would be entitled to find that they had acted negligently. The Act would also oblige professional bodies to consider the Code when determining whether a practitioner had been guilty of professional misconduct. Departure from its terms would give rise to a ground for complaint, although this would not be conclusive and professionals would have the opportunity to justify their actions.

As has been shown, it is not possible to provide an absolute right to specific treatments, but the position of patients can be improved by establishing fair procedures. These should be set out in the Code of Patients' Rights and should follow the principles elaborated by Galligan in Chapter 2. The Code should state, for example, that individual patients denied access to treatment or the specific type of care they want are entitled to an explanation. This would apply to major decisions, such as being refused an operation, as well as to more mundane problems such as access to incontinence aids or the right of patients to smoke in hospital. Where the explanations are unsatisfactory, a complaint could be brought under the new complaints procedure. Managerial decisions which adversely affect an individual's chances of receiving care, such as the reduction of services, would also be within the scope of the complaints procedure.

In addition, all contracts and arrangements for patient services within the health service, including those with GPs and dentists, should incorporate a commitment to work in accordance with the Code. Failure to do so would give rise to the possibility of remedial action by managers through disciplinary proceedings and/or the withholding of payment. This would be in addition to any action by aggrieved health service users.

Private health-care facilities, such as nursing homes, would also be required to incorporate the principles set out in the Code into their operation and continued registration under the Registered Homes Act 1984 would be con-ditional on their doing so.

The Patient's Charter of 1991

The Conservative Government's *Patient's Charter*, issued late in 1991, shares some of the characteristics of our proposals. For example, it requires health authorities to publish targets for waiting times. However, it fails to achieve our objectives in a number of ways. First, it assumes that the existing law governing consent and confidentiality is satisfactory. As we have already argued, reform of these areas is necessary to protect the rights of patients. Second, it takes a different view of what constitutes a right from that which we have adopted. This can be seen in the approach to the right to a second opinion. The *Patient's Charter* considers that the fact that your GP can prevent you seeking a second opinion does not prevent you having a right. We do not accept that: it leaves the power in the hands of professionals and fails to increase patient choice. Our proposal is that patients be able to require local health authorities to arrange for a second opinion even against the wishes of the GP. The *Patient's Charter* sets out standards against which services are to be measured, but again this fails to adopt our approach to rights. The standards impose duties on officials, but do nothing to empower patients. As such they are more a management tool than an enhancement of the position of patients.

More importantly however, the Conservative Government's *Patient's Charter* fails to address the difficulties of enforcement. It identifies complaints procedures as one of the three new rights to be introduced, but gives no details of how they will operate. The most concrete reference to enforcement instructs those who believe that their 'Charter Rights' have been denied to seek redress from the Chief Executive of the NHS. In fact, it is enforcement that raises the most problems. Without a proper scheme for redress, any charter, however detailed, would have little impact on the position of patients. The final section of this chapter discusses our proposals for a web of enforcement mechanisms designed to ensure that patients can vindicate their rights. It is the omission of such discussion that constitutes the most significant weakness of the Conservatives' proposals.

Future developments

It is important that any framework for realising health rights should be flexible. Public health needs are bound to change, patients' expectations may increase. New technology may enable further progress. Issues of health policy and patients' rights need to be kept under review. Responsibility for general review of quality and access to services has been given to the new Clinical Standards Advisory Group by the 1990 Act. To be satisfactory, this Group needs to have significant non-professional representation. It is also necessary to extend the remit of the Group, or perhaps to set up a separate body, to include the ethical and social implications of possible new developments.[18] The initiative of the Nuffield Foundation, which has recently set up such a body, might provide a basis for a future official committee. Medical technology is a rapidly developing field and changes in practice cannot be allowed to prejudice the interests of the community. In the past public debate has come too late to assist scientists and health professionals to meet such challenges in a responsible manner.

Enforcement of rights to health care

The mechanisms by which health-care rights are enforced need to perform a number of functions. They must enable grievances to be aired, challenge unsatisfactory practice, prevent the recurrence of mishaps, compensate the victims of accidents, deter practitioners from allowing standards to slip. There is a wide variety of existing mechanisms for responding to untoward incidents.[19] This is a product of diverse historical origins rather than conscious choice and reform should aim to streamline it so far as is compatible with performing all the functions.

This section discusses three aspects of the task: complaints procedures, professional discipline and compensation schemes. Its main focus is on the first. A brief treatment of the others is included to establish where the complaints procedures would fit into the overall framework for enforcement.

Complaints procedures

Confidence in a complaints system can be achieved only if it is independent of the relevant health authorities and professional bodies against which complaints can be made. Confidence in health services can only be maintained if users are satisfied that effective procedures exist to ensure good practice. An improved complaints procedure is therefore in the interests of patients and professionals. The new system should be comprehensive, covering clinical and non-clinical complaints and extending not only to hospitals but also to primary and community care.

Fair but informal procedures will help to reduce the element of confrontation. The system should allow both for the complaints to press their complaint themselves, and for them to hand it over to the relevant investigating body (the local complaints officer or the Health Service Commissioners). This would permit complaints to be brought to prevent the recurrence of malpractice even where the complainant does not wish to pursue a personal grievance. It would also permit relatives or staff to raise in confidence matters about which they are concerned, and to leave the investigator to initiate enquiries. Clearly, the complainant and those complained against must have the chance to explain themselves. Assistance, but not legal representation, should be allowed for all parties.

Existing NHS complaints procedures are unnecessarily complex and insufficiently comprehensive. The new complaints procedure should provide for a two-tier system, partly modelled on certain features of the current system – on the handling of hospital complaints at a local level and on the work of the Health Service Commissioners at a national level. District health authorities should continue to designate officers in each hospital to handle complaints. Family health service authorities should do the same for each practice area. These officers should *not* be drawn from the health professions. To protect their independence, their appointment and removal would be subject to the approval of the Health Service Commissioners. (We do not propose direct appointment of local commissioners, as it would be expensive and increase the formality of the procedures at the expense of both complainants and health service staff.)

The existing restriction of clinical matters to exclusively professional scrutiny cannot continue. The absence of lay involvement undermines rather than enhances trust in the professions. There is no difference in the basis of the complaint, which is that the professional has failed to satisfy the right of the patient to proper respect and consideration. The Code of Patients' Rights will provide the standards against which complaints are judged. Since matters relating to clinical judgement raise technical issues, the investigator should enlist the assistance of a paid assessor with relevant expertise. But once this advice has been received, the professional's conduct can be evaluated by lay people.

The jurisdiction of the Health Service Commissioners should be expanded to cover clinical judgment and also complaints against GPs. They should also be able to initiate investigations without receiving a complaint. These extensions of the Commissioners' powers have already been recommended by the Parliamentary Select Committee responsible for overseeing the Commissioners' work, but they have not been effected. With these reforms in place, the Commissioners would be able to handle complaints from all areas of the NHS. Where local investigators have reason to believe that an inquiry should be initiated, they would be obliged to inform the Commissioners.

It is vital that the complaints procedure should be publicised to service users. All hospitals should be required to provide patients with details of the complaints system and how to contact the relevant person. GPs should provide the same material in patient information booklets. (Withholding information deters people from complaining.) Mechanisms will have to be set up for those who need help to articulate their claims. Advocacy services and agencies inspecting and monitoring standards should be required to draw problems to the attention of the Health Service Commissioners. These problems could then be brought within the complaints procedures through the Commissioners' powers of independent investigation.

Complainants would normally go first to the relevant local officer who would explore the possibility of dealing with the complaint informally. If the complainant wished to bring a formal complaint, without or after an informal procedure, the local officer would normally carry out the investigation. Serious cases, at present referred to the district health authority, would under the new system go directly to the Commissioners.

Direct access to the Commissioners would also be available, but complaints could be referred back to the relevant local officer if appropriate. In order to facilitate 'whistle-blowing', direct access to the Commissioners would be the normal channel for health service employees, and confidentiality would be assured. The Commissioners would be able to use the power to initiate investigations to avoid identifying informants.

A complaints procedure is judged largely by results. A full report of each finding should always be given to the complainant, person(s) complained about and the relevant health authority. Under the current procedures this is not guaranteed. The investigator should be entitled to demand action (including compensation) by the persons and bodies complained against. Compliance should be monitored, and failure to do so reported to the Health Service Commissioners, who may decide to initiate another inquiry into the reasons for non-compliance.

The original complainant should have the right to receive a copy of the report on compliance, on request from the investigator. Appeal against any order made by a local investigator would be available to the Health Service Commissioners, whose decision would be final. The work of the Commissioners would remain subject to the general supervision of the Parliamentary Select Committee.

This complaints procedure would apply within all areas of National Health Service care. The point of entry to the system would be local. The workings of the system and the standards against which it operated would be uniform. It would therefore be simpler, as well as more effective, than the existing avenues for processing complaints.

As far as possible, it should be extended to cover private health care. This could be done by ensuring, under the supervision of the Health Service Commissioners, that independent complaints mechanisms are a precondition of registration. The practice of individual professionals acting privately can probably only be directly supervised through the relevant professional body. If, however, they are working at a hospital, nursing home or clinic which is subject to the registration system, they should be covered by the necessary complaints procedure.

Professional bodies

The existence of professional registers with restricted entry ensures that those who claim expertise possess at least minimum qualifications. But qualifications do not guarantee continuing competence. The system of professional regulation therefore needs to maintain and improve standards as well as entry requirements. This can be done in a number of ways. Professional disciplinary proceedings can remove incompetent practitioners from the register. There are procedures to check the health of professionals and to suspend the registration of those who are too sick to reach the standards required for safe practice. Requirements for continuing professional education, such as those being explored by the nursing profession, may go further towards maintaining high standards.

Removing practitioners from the register due to ill health or disciplinary offenses is an important means by which the public can be protected from unsatisfactory practitioners. The regulatory systems operated by each of the health-care professions differ in detail and some of these differences should be removed. The first area for reform is membership of the professional bodies. Self-regulation in its purest form is no longer acceptable. All professions, except for medicine, already have representatives of other professions on their governing body and so promote the exchange of professional ideas and skills. In addition, there should be increased lay involvement from outside the health-care professions, specifically from Health Service users. Currently the 'lay' members of professional bodies may come from other professions within the health-care services rather than from outside. Lay participation should also be ensured on the committees with responsibility for issuing guidance on professional standards and hearing disciplinary proceedings. These changes should be required by the Rights of Patients Act. Membership could continue to be predominantly – but not exclusively – professional.

Currently, the basis on which the professions assess allegations of disciplinary offences varies. Some, such as nurses, examine complaints of 'professional misconduct'. Others, such as doctors, are only prepared to consider 'serious professional misconduct'. The relevant legislation should be amended by the Rights of Patients Act to adopt the lower threshold. This would not require all those guilty of misconduct to be struck off, but would give the professional bodies the power and duty to oversee their practice. Some further guidance as to the meaning of misconduct should be given. It should be made clear by the new Act that a single incident may constitute misconduct and that whistle-blowing cannot constitute misconduct in the form of an attack on a colleague's reputation. The Code of Patients' Rights will play a key role in setting standards for professional conduct.

Professional bodies should also take a more active role. They should be entitled to initiate investigations on the basis of confidential complaints. This would help draw attention to incompetent practitioners. Registrars should be required by the Rights of Patients Act to record all complaints, and the practice of any practitioner who is the subject of repeated complaints should be investigated. The professional body would then be in a position to consider the practitioner's practice as a whole and judge their overall competence and not merely respond to individual allegations in a vacuum. This would allow practitioners who consistently fall below acceptable standards, but who do so on each occasion in only a small way, to be disciplined. In such cases the professional bodies would be expected to use their powers constructively to make continued registration conditional on good practice or even additional training.

Compensation

However high the quality of health care, there will always be accidents in the course of its delivery. The existing compensation system, based primarily on the tort of negligence, is widely acknowledged to be unsatisfactory. The main purposes of tort law have been described as compensation and deterrence. The current system fails on both counts. As a system of compensation, it is expensive to operate, and much of the money paid out by the Health Service in compensation is eaten up by legal costs. The need to prove negligence means that many of those who need financial assistance are not able to get it. Many actions are settled out of court so that the true facts often never come to light. The reluctance of the judges to challenge professional wisdom reduces the value of litigation as a means of establishing standards. The fact that damages are not usually paid by the professional, but by defence societies or health authorities, reduces the deterrent effect on individual practitioners.

Improved standards and deterrence of their breach can be achieved through the Code of Patients' Rights and the new complaints procedure. This system may lead to compensation, but its main objective is to investigate what went wrong. Recent proposals for no-fault compensation schemes have raised objections from user groups mainly on the ground that they do not include proper systems of accountability.[20] The measures outlined in this chapter would satisfy the need for better accountability and enable the victims of accidents to find out what went wrong. It will be easier to evaluate proposals for a new compensation scheme once these measures have been put into practice.

No-fault compensation schemes in Sweden and New Zealand are often proposed as models, but these exclude some people who need financial assistance – for two main reasons. First, the criteria for eligibility require some sort of mishap arising from treatment and therefore exclude cases arising from disease or from genuine accidents. Second, the need to prove a causal link between the mishap and the injury excludes even some of those who may have suffered their injury in the required manner, but where the cause cannot be certain.

Much depends on what compensation is supposed to be for. If a person's basic needs (for example, for adequate health care and a living wage) are not being met – whether as a result of malpractice, negligence, mishap, disease or accident – then the solution should lie with the welfare system itself, not with a compensation scheme. Where compensation is sought not for basic needs, but for loss of capacity above this level, there may be a stronger case for having to prove that someone is at fault in order to win damages. The existing system, in which professional negligence must be established, is generous to the health professions, especially perhaps to doctors.[21] However, if other reforms outlined above were in place, a fault-based compensation scheme might prove more satisfactory than a no fault system.[22]

Conclusion

This chapter has covered a wide range of issues, all of which arise from the idea of taking health rights seriously. As we have shown, a number of conceptual and political matters must be considered before health rights can be defined. All deserve longer treatment than was possible here, but an extended theoretical discussion could have obscured many of the practical problems of implementing health rights. This chapter has therefore sought to be specific enough to provide concrete proposals for a rights-based approach to health. In the long term, the success of such a strategy should be assessed by its contribution to a change in the culture of health services: a culture in which patients' rights are respected, with little need for recourse through the courts or complaints procedures, would be the greatest achievement.

6 RIGHTS AND SOCIAL WORK

Nina Biehal, Mike Fisher, Peter Marsh, Eric Sainsbury

The word citizenship has been employed by parties across the political spectrum in current debates about welfare. One model is that of the 'active citizen' which emphasises personal rather than public responsibilities for care. Another model is a citizenship of rights and entitlement to welfare, recognising the relative powerlessness of welfare users and the inadequacy of consumerism as a principle of state welfare provision.

These conflicting interpretations of citizenship are prominent in debates about community care. In recent years, the traditional social work values of respect for individuals and the right to self-determination have been translated into the language of the marketplace. The user of social services is regarded as a customer choosing between a range of options on offer from public, private and voluntary agencies. All this is couched in the language of participation and choice, obscuring the fact that these 'consumers' are likely to be poor, vulnerable, perhaps isolated, and rarely in a position to 'shop around' or 'take their custom elsewhere'. This notion of the citizen as consumer also obscures the tension between the legislation on community care and the broader political strategy of limiting the powers of local government. The language of diversity and choice, with social services departments acting as managers rather than providers of services, is linked to a reduction in the public provision of social services. Local authorities are required to encourage the provision of services by private and voluntary agencies, with the public sector providing only residual services to the most stigmatised groups, such as the most severely disabled.[1]

However, the language of participation, choice and (in the Children Act 1989) partnership, is also employed by those concerned with the genuine empowerment of welfare users. Many users of social services are excluded from full citizenship. Their right to treatment as equals may be limited by poverty, racism, assumptions about gender, age and disability. They often have no alternative but to depend on the decisions of welfare professionals, who control access to resources and exercise professional discretion about the use of these resources. A commitment to the rights of users of social services requires careful consideration of the ways in which social-work practice may actually disempower people. By defining people's needs for them, making decisions on their behalf and denying them responsibility through the exercise of professional discretion, current practice may serve as a barrier to entitlement to welfare, just as poverty is a barrier in the private sector.

If social services and other public departments are to address the relative powerlessness of the individuals who use them, then services must be accessible to all (regardless of ethnic origin, language, disability). Users of these services need adequate information about eligibility, decision making and complaints procedures. Crucially, there should be opportunities to participate in decision making at every level: in policy development, service planning, the management of day care and residential units and in the contacts between individuals and social-services workers. This chapter deals with the last of these levels. It suggests that the commitment to participation, choice and partnership must be translated into a clear set of rights at the level of social-work practice. Otherwise, these terms can function as little more than slogans and will fail to challenge the 'false consumerist democracy of the market'.[2]

One of the difficulties for social work in establishing its credentials is that there are substantial similarities between what social workers do and what, at some level, we all do – talk to people and try to offer assistance, support and protection. Since it sometimes appears as though we could all do social work, it might also appear that we don't need special groups of people with special training to do the job. There are differences, however, and they are important to the question of establishing the rights of users.

Social workers often work with groups of people who receive markedly less assistance, support and protection from society than others, and there is a need to devote specific services to groups of people who may be seen as unpopular or undeserving. Social workers also work with groups of people whose needs are so great that their immediate network of kin and friends just can't cope. For people whose resources are severely stretched, it can be important to be able to turn to someone without incurring a reciprocal obligation, and here it helps that there are people paid to offer assistance, support and protection. There are also circumstances where special powers are used to interfere in the lives of others, usually to protect children and other dependent family members: exercising these powers requires specialist knowledge and properly conferred legal authority.

Needs and social work practice

Meeting needs is a professed aim of social workers and other professionals; and current legislation and the accompanying guidelines support the view that services should be 'needs-led'. However, defining need should be a process of negotiation, rather than one of discovery: that is, people's needs emerge from discussion and through the exercise of professional understanding rather than by being detectable through some objective test, and must involve the user's definition in order to be sure of the accuracy and relevance of provision. This raises three issues which must be clarified before we can sustain a coherent position on the rights of service users: first, distinguishing need and want; second, recognising that some needs are more important than others; third, determining who has the right to define whose needs.

People want many things, not all of which would be properly thought of as 'needs' and met through public services. The act of professional assessment must attempt to distinguish need from want, and must also be free from moralistic judgement which implies either that people don't really know what they need or that they typically focus on what they want rather than on what they need. In defining the rights of users in specific cases, therefore, workers and users should discuss whether a request for help is in response to a want or a need, the user's feelings about the urgency of the situation, the possible effects of not meeting the request in the short and long terms, and the ambiguities between wanting and needing. The worker will no doubt have views about the importance of certain requests for help, and about the consequences of meeting or not meeting these requests. Thus, the process of shifting from 'want' to 'felt need' and to 'expressed need' will be differently conceptualized by individual workers as well as by individual users. It is, therefore, a skilled job to promote equity of provision in the context of differences in perceptions of urgency and consequences. The obvious risk, when thinking about rights, is that the pursuit of equity in resource allocation and the professional judgements of workers may obscure individual differences in the experience of need. The future separation of assessment from service provisions (NHS and Community Care Act) may help to prevent this, but the risk will remain of overlooking the sense in which every citizen is an expert in defining his/her own needs.

Two further matters should be mentioned. First, there will always be occasions where the worker will have to negotiate in the context of a shortage of resources. Second, there will always be occasions where one person's expressed needs conflict with the needs of others. Thus, the process of workers negotiating with users about the 'legitimacy' of a need is central both to the maintenance of users' rights and to the accountability of workers.

Some needs have higher priority than others in the eyes of users and workers alike: adequate food and shelter, for example, have priority over certain possessions and social relationships in terms of survival. In the perspective of the user, however, priority is not necessarily the same as importance, and users may want attention to some needs for reasons which don't appear to be related to their importance in, for example, keeping them well or able to cope independently. Workers should therefore discuss both priority and importance. Differences in prioritisation among users and workers are sometimes overlooked: workers tend to give priority to the needs that interest them or that they feel they can meet, rather than to needs which – in other people's judgement – should assume higher priority.

Needs will be differently defined by the service-user, the worker, the relative or neighbour and by 'public opinion'. Sustaining the rights of users is primarily based on negotiating between these perspectives, particularly those of user and worker. But the opinions of relatives or neighbours or of the wider public can have adverse effects on the wellbeing of users or on the achievement of desirable outcomes and, if so, workers have an obligation to try to influence these opinions. A consequence of this is that workers must adopt a critical stance towards legislation, professional and administrative processes and decisions where these, though reflecting majority public or political viewpoints, impede effective negotiation of needs and the provision of relevant services.

In spotlighting the exchanges between the user and the worker, we are aware that it is difficult to disentangle the different threads of how need is defined, problems identified, information given and choice and participation secured. In writing on each of these, we may sometimes give the impression that they can be considered as distinct areas, capable of being implemented in a self-contained way. This is not our experience. For example, the concept that users define their own needs must be connected to their right to have information on what services might be available: otherwise users will limit themselves to what they know about. Further, the self-definition of need must be seen as the first step in a series of negotiations about service, in all of which the user has the right to informed and significant participation. A central part of our argument about rights for users of social-work services is therefore that agencies must have a complete and thorough-going 'user-orientation', a philosophy and a practice which permeates service activities and constantly underlines the connections between rights to define problems, information, choice and participation.

In proposing a set of rights for users of social services, we recognise that these can only be crude tools. There is a danger of introducing either a paper manifesto, ideologically sound but practically worthless, or else just another set of procedural guidelines, honoured to the letter but enacted without commitment. Professional practice is rarely improved through ideological or procedural sermonising, and there is a substantial difference for the user between, for example, attending a case conference because an agency procedure requires it and doing so when all present believe it is the user's right. It is the difference between, in the first case, going through the motions and, in the second, being positively welcomed as a partner with a unique contribution.

A statement of rights cannot guarantee changes in professional practice.

Our view is that it is nevertheless valuable for three reasons. First, it sets out for public scrutiny the agency philosophy governing service; second, it sets some targets (albeit procedural ones) for practice and clarifies the standards that social workers are expected to achieve; third – and most importantly – it provides an external reference point for the exchanges between workers and clients. Our intention is that the statement of rights should provide a framework for users' negotiations, balancing public accountability against the power of professionals.

In the rest of this chapter, we highlight issues in defining problems, in making agreements with clients which respect choice, and in participation in decision-making. After defining these issues, we present brief evidence drawn from a research and development project ('Social Work In Partnership', Universities of Bradford and Sheffield, funded by the Joseph Rowntree Foundation) designed to explore ways of implementing partnership with social services users. Finally, we present proposals about users' rights and how they might be enacted in practice.

Defining problems

The Issue

The question of who defines the problems to which social services respond critically affects users' rights. Do individuals who use social services have the opportunity to participate in defining their own problems and the needs which arise from these?

The problem

Participation in decision-making begins with the definition of problems, since it is the way in which people's problems are defined which determines the solutions offered to them. We should be clear about the difference between the process of defining problems and the process of agreeing a service. Workers may believe that they encourage people to participate in decision-making, when at the outset they may already have set a narrow agenda based solely on their own professional assessment. If the individuals who use social services are not encouraged and assisted in defining their problems, their own view of their problems and preferred solutions may be marginalised or ignored.

Professionals do not always ask open-ended questions about a person's own view of their problems but may simply ask them to respond to questions about specific pre-defined issues. These questions may be based on the worker's preconceptions about the 'category' of problem, while the individual's own view remains unexplored. This may be especially problematic for people from minority ethnic groups, since a professional's response may be based on generalisations about their cultural background rather than on an exploration of their own views about their particular problems.[3] While it is, of course, entirely proper for workers to draw on their knowledge and professional experience, a distinction must be made between this and the practice of basing assessments on assumptions or on routine responses.

> *Example*: A family whose children's names were on the Child
> Protection Register was considered by the social worker to have the
> 'standard problems you would expect in a family where the father is
> unemployed and there are four children under five'. The father was
> preoccupied with his marital problems but said he had not discussed
> these with his social worker 'because she didn't ask'.

Often, professionals do not disclose their assumptions about the problems they consider individuals to be experiencing and about what they hope to achieve by offering particular services. Not only does this leave people confused, but it makes it impossible for them to challenge the worker's view of their problems if they do not agree with it. What is required is an open discussion between professionals and users of social services about the way in which each party views the problems to be addressed, the kinds of help that users would like and the kinds of help that professionals consider appropriate. Only by sharing their assessment with the individuals concerned can workers empower them to act as partners in defining their own problems and solutions, openly negotiating with the worker where there are areas of disagreement. They may want the worker to act as an advocate on their behalf, or to offer practical assistance or counselling. Frequently, workers consider themselves to be offering counselling because they perceive a need for this, but the individuals concerned may be unaware of this and can in no sense be said to have chosen this type of service. Even in situations where the worker may be legally obliged to intervene in a particular way (for example, by taking children into care) it should be possible to make clear to people where there may still be scope for negotiation about the type of help they receive.

> *Example*: An elderly woman was extremely puzzled by her social
> worker's refusal to act as an advocate on her behalf in her dealings
> with the Housing Department and with health professionals. The social
> worker felt she should be encouraged to undertake these negotiations
> herself as she did not want to encourage dependency, but had not
> shared the rationale for her actions. Instead of discussing with the
> elderly woman what degree of independent action she herself wished to
> take and in which areas of her life, the social worker's approach
> imposed an ideal of independence on her which was not open to
> negotiation.

Workers are sometimes under pressure to fit people's problems into the particular services their departments can provide. They often feel constrained to conceptualise an individual's unique set of problems as a need for the available services – for day care, a short stay in a children's home, a home help or meals on wheels. The individual's or family's particular problems are conceptualised in terms which dovetail neatly with the framework of existing organisational boundaries and which are consistent with service availability. Service-oriented assessments are administratively convenient but pay scant attention to the individual's own conception of their problems. There has been much discussion of this issue in the field of community care, where many have argued that a more flexible and imaginative response is required.[4] Resource shortages or administrative structures may lead professionals to suggest to service users that the service being offered is the most appropriate response to their particular problems, when it is in fact the only one they are able to provide at the time.

> *Example*: A teenage boy and his mother were told that the best way to deal with their problems would be to place the boy in a children's home. This was offered to them as the best option for their specific needs (although the mother felt that foster care would be more helpful) whereas in fact it was the only option that the department could provide at the time. The worker commented 'I don't like working in this way because I am constrained by the department who in turn are limited by financial restrictions'.

Not only are people's problems viewed in terms of organisational boundaries within a social services department, but the limits to the help offered are often set by the boundaries between that agency and others, such as the health service, the DSS or housing agencies. Co-operation between agencies is often poor, with the result that service-led assessments are often limited to the services available within one agency rather than across a range of agencies. Yet people's problems frequently do not divide neatly into categories that fit the boundaries and solutions of each particular agency.

Where users of social services also require help from other agencies, there is a danger that in the process of defining problems the user's voice is further marginalised in the negotiations between professionals on their behalf. The complexity of negotiating with a range of agencies can be quite overwhelming and people often turn to social workers to act as advocates for them with other professionals. Social workers need to liaise with other professionals, both from their own department and from other agencies, through informal contacts and through the formal processes of case conferences, reviews and planning meetings. Yet where several professionals are involved, there is a real risk that the user's own view of the problem is marginalised with precedence being given to more powerful voices.

However, eliciting a person's own view of their problems may not always be straightforward. People who use social services may edit their account of their needs in line with their assumptions about the type of help that is likely to be available. Older people who are worried about their ability to cope might be reluctant to list the problems they are experiencing. They may need a great deal of support and encouragement before they can express their concerns without undermining their confidence. In addition, both older people and the parents of children at risk may minimise the significance of problems because they fear that workers may take unwanted action 'on their behalf'.

Where people are considered to be at risk or are otherwise involuntary users of social services (such as the parents of some children at risk) their own view of their problems is particularly likely to be overlooked. The worker's concern about risk may lead them to impose their own definitions of the individual's or family's needs without negotiation. Workers may selectively seek service users' views only in non-contentious areas of their lives rather than on the issues which are the principal cause for social services involvement, such as violent behaviour or the abuse of children. Or workers may start by focusing on users' views but jettison this approach if there is an increase in what they consider to be deviant behaviour, imposing their own assessment of the situation without negotiation. They may also go through the motions of eliciting a person's view but then ignore it and offer help only with problems that the worker considers important. In situations where people are considered at risk or in some way deviant there is a greater likelihood that 'Some needs are formally translated into rights and informally denied'.[5]

> *Example*: In a family where the teenage son's violent behaviour was
> causing problems, the worker began by helping the family to focus on
> the problems as each of them saw them. Only minor problems were
> dealt with at this stage. However, following an outburst of violent
> behaviour by the son the worker dropped this approach and,
> conceptualising the family as not knowing their own needs, he imposed
> a care plan without involving them in formulating it.

There are also occasions when people approach social services for help with specific problems, only to find that social workers have not only redefined their problems for them but have included additional problems on the agenda without negotiation. They may not have requested help with these additional problems and the social worker may have no legal mandate for intervention. This often takes the form of the worker imposing conditions on individuals without either seeking their agreement or making explicit any legal authority for doing so. In these circumstances, workers may be motivated by a quite proper concern about risk and may be seeking the best care for a child. However, what is at issue is the fact that they have imposed these conditions without making it clear to the people concerned whether or not there is a legal basis for them.

Example: A young woman, living at home with her parents, placed her child in voluntary care at birth. A few weeks later she requested the return of her baby. The social worker insisted that she had to find independent accommodation and furnish it appropriately before the return of the child could be considered. The mother experienced the imposition of these conditions as an obstacle course that had been set for her by her social worker.

Proposals in relation to people's rights to define problems

(1) People should have a right to be involved in the process of defining their needs. They should be given whatever assistance is necessary to help them define their own problems and needs and to prioritise them. If their definition of need does not coincide with the worker's, they should have the right to negotiate an agreed list of problems to be worked on instead of having the worker's definition of their problems imposed on them. Workers should make clear their reasons for not assisting with some needs that an individual might express, for example where these might conflict with the needs of dependent others.

(2) People should have the right to be treated as partners in the assessment process. Workers should share their assumptions about the individual family's problems with them as a basis for negotiation about the course of action to be taken.

(3) People should have the right to be told about the worker's role and powers in a specific situation, that is, to know what the worker has come for (or about).

(4) People should have the right to give explicit consent to or refuse investigation of problems, except in situations where the worker has statutory responsibilities. These responsibilities may require a worker to make an assessment if there is an indication that, for example, a child is at risk.

(5) People should have the right to give explicit consent or to refuse intervention (except where this conflicts with the rights of dependent others or there is a legal mandate to intervene).

(6) People from minority ethnic groups should have a right to receive information about services in their first language. At every stage in the process of assessment and review they should have the option of having a worker who speaks their first language to enable them to express their own view of their problems.

(7) People from minority ethnic groups should have the right to a full exploration of their individual needs. They should not have their problems defined for them by professionals on the basis of assumptions about their cultural norms.

Agreements and choice

The issue

It may seem irrelevant to argue that services should be based on agreement and choice: policy and practice appear to enshrine these concepts anyway. Our point is, however, that the policy of agreements fails to reflect the involuntary nature of much contact between users and services, and that the practice of workers is often based on coercion and constraint rather than on agreement. The way existing policy and practice is conceptualised needs to be challenged if users' rights to intervention based on agreement and choice are to become a reality.

The problem

In the redefinition of social welfare engendered by the NHS and Community Care Act 1990 and by the Children Act 1989, the language of consumers, users, service agreements, partnership, choice and empowerment is used to describe the future basis of intervention. At the same time, workers claim that their practice is in any case founded on negotiation and consent. It may appear from this that all politicians and managers need to do is provide the context to permit workers to enact the philosophy of 'consumer' involvement.

In reality, however, there are several problems with the application of agreements to the majority of social services' work. Agreement as a concept implies a voluntary user, actively seeking service: in contrast, most social services' work involves people who would rather not be users, people obliged to seek help through poverty or disability, or people obliged to receive help because someone else (a court or a local authority) says they are not able to care for themselves or for their children. In these circumstances, the users cannot be categorised as 'free to choose' to use services and any subsequent 'agreement' made with them must be viewed in this light.

> *Example*: A family was under pressure to make arrangements for the care of two pre-school children. The mother was abusing drugs and the father was about to begin a long period of working away from home. The social workers made it clear to both parents that the children remaining with the mother in the father's absence was not acceptable and that steps would be taken to prevent this. The parents eventually 'agreed' to the children going to live with their grandparents.
>
> *Example*: An older man was leaving hospital after minor in-patient treatment and wanted to return home. A relative who would have had to offer substantial care was unwilling to do so. After some negotiation, the older man 'agreed' to enter a residential home for a trial period. Later, it was agreed that he did not need the services of

the residential home but his relative was still unwilling to offer the substantial care he would need to return to his own home. He wanted to go home without having to receive domiciliary services, but eventually he 'agreed' and returned home.

A second problem in applying agreements to social services' work is that the formal guarantee of voluntariness enshrined in some current legislation in fact masks a substantial degree of coercion. For example, admission to an Old People's Home under the National Assistance Act 1948 requires an application by the older person to her local authority: it is supposed to be a voluntary action. However, it is not unusual to find little evidence of a positive choice having been made by the 'applicant'. A positive choice might be possible if alternatives were considered, but a study of applicants showed that 23 per cent considered they had not received information about alternatives.[6] A recent study of the operation of the Mental Health Act 1983 shows that almost 14 per cent of requests to detain a person under compulsion in hospital resulted in that person being admitted informally or retaining their informal status.[7] It is difficult to call these admissions 'voluntary', or to suggest that the user had 'agreed' to stay in hospital, if the alternative was the use of compulsion.

Perhaps the most serious difficulty, however, concerns social work practice itself. As we have argued, workers resist giving clients a free rein to define their own problems and this will affect agreements made about what to do. The very familiarity with the concept of agreement may mask the extent to which practice needs to change in order to implement it. Workers' current practice is to use agreements defined more by the worker than by the client, in the form of verbal understandings rather than written documents to which reference may be made, and which are often rather vaguely defined so that it is difficult to know when any single goal has been reached. Such 'agreements' may also permit the worker to add elements unilaterally, so that the user experiences an escalating series of conditions of involvement.

Example: A mother of a young child on the child protection register was 'allowed' to continue care on the basis of breaking off a relationship with a man convicted of sexual offences against children. She subsequently began a new relationship. The social services' department made deregistration dependent on obtaining new housing and establishing a stable family unit.

Users who are obliged to be in contact with social services do not in these circumstances have the option not to be a client. They must stay in contact and abide by the 'agreed' terms until a decision is taken to alter the terms to permit the user to discontinue contact – a form of involvement which it is difficult to characterise as being based on 'agreement'.

Many of these arguments apply equally to the concept of choice. Often choice is seen exclusively in terms of whether there is more than one alternative resource or service the user may receive. But choice must be thought of as embracing a much wider variety of issues if it is to reflect the right to have some say about services. Choice must, for instance, take account of whether a user can choose not to receive any service at all. This is often not the case, and all users may be offered is a 'choice' between obligatory types of interventions rather than whether to remain in contact with social services. As we have argued, users often feel they have little choice over which of their problems come to the attention of social services and how they are defined. Ethnic minority users experience very little choice about the language in which information is conveyed to them, or about the ethnicity of the worker allocated to them.

There are special issues concerning older people, who may feel they are being hurried into defining a set of problems at a pace not of their choosing. Older people in particular find it hard to make a range of needs explicit. If you don't know what is available, you don't know what to ask for and the tendency for many older people is to keep quiet. We have examples of sensitive workers carefully retreating from requiring older people to be specific about their needs, in recognition of the necessity to provide information and space before they can be expressed. Careful work is also required to counsel older people about their right to services, in circumstances where their own background and media pressure can lead them to regard public services as unwelcome charity.

There are also special issues concerning carers. There may be a case for having a special type of agreement with carers which allows implicit recognition rather than explicit statement of the need for emotional support. This finding arises from studying instances where the workers offer emotional support, and have it accepted by the carers, without any prior discussion or recording of this as a 'need'. Several factors are at work here, of which perhaps the most important is the sense in which carers are colleagues as well as potential users. It follows that the style of service must be arranged to minimise any requirement for the carer to become a 'user'.

Last, of course, choice about services is often reduced to the absolute minimum by shortage of resources. If a service needed is not available, there is a tendency for workers to present what is available in the best possible light. Users perceive such 'choices' as little more than the opportunity to exercise a veto, in the knowledge that to do so runs the risk of alienating the one possible source of help.

Proposals in relation to people's rights to agreement - based work and to choice

(1) People should have the right to know by what authority social services intervene in their lives, to know whether they are obliged by law to receive

intervention or whether they are free to discontinue contact. People are entitled to know what they are required to do by virtue of the legal authority vested in social services departments, and what by virtue of professional expectation or procedural custom, as well as what is negotiable and what not. This information should be available in written form as well as verbally.

(2) Where people become involved in procedures to which their explicit consent is required, they have the right to expect that workers will seek it thoroughly and record it formally. They should also have the right to expect workers to avoid any form of coercion to achieve 'voluntary' consent.

(3) People should have the right to a formal written agreement, supplemented verbally, describing tasks to be undertaken, assigning responsibility and including an estimated timescale. The language used should be related to the people's words and concepts, and translation or interpretation should be arranged if required. Where tasks are required of people by legal authority, their compliance in these should not be described as the result of agreement.

(4) People should have the right to state their preferences as to the age, sex and ethnicity of the worker who gives them service, to expect every effort to be made to meet these preferences and an explanation of the reasons where this is not possible.

(5) People should have the right to expect workers to assess carefully how much information they possess about services and to ensure they are not hampered from making their needs explicit by lack of knowledge about available services.

(6) Unless there is a clear and communicated legal authority requiring otherwise, people have the right to expect workers to allow them to define their problems at a pace and in a manner comfortable to them and to reserve as private issues they do not wish to present for assessment.

(7) People should be told and have access to a written copy of the worker's report about what services are required so that they can then judge whether the services offered match the assessment.

(8) People who are offered a single 'option' should be given information about why they are not being offered a choice.

Participation

The issue

People cannot fully participate as of right unless they are involved in decisions affecting them. Three critical stages of contact with social services are entry and eligibility, initial service decisions, and the continuing decisions which can include people's experience of services. You could refer to these stages as getting into the system, deciding on services at the start, and deciding on services in the light of user experience.

The problem

Social services are, by their nature, individual and personal and there will be few, if any, situations where decisions can be taken without some user involvement. It is also clear that services are more effective if linked to a participative style of work[8] and if the user is actively participating in the work.[9] There have been continuing calls within social work and social care for the ethical basis of service to include user participation, as in, for example, the aptly entitled report 'Clients are Fellow Citizens'.[10]

However, the practice of social work has often fallen short of these ideals, and participation has been low in quantity and quality.[11,12] The government has sought to enhance collaboration by introducing new policies on, for example, access to records,[13,14] and to produce greater participation in decisions about contact between parents and children in care.[15] The Children Act 1989 and the NHS and Community Care Act 1990 will encourage participation even further.

Why don't workers therefore encourage these elements of participation? Part of the reason is that the three critical stages (entry and eligibility, initial service decisions, and continuing decisions) appear in a rather different guise for the worker. They are likely to be referred to by workers and agencies as investigation, assessment and review. These terms imply that the worker is active and the user passive during the three stages. Currently dominant models of practice emphasise this active worker/passive user model[16] and this is partly the reason why a gap exists between policy and practice. But there is also a gap because of the role of social work in controlling behaviour judged to be harmful to others. Social work is regularly concerned with decisions about whether individuals need protection from harm. In these cases, the worker is more active in the sense that individuals must be subject to these processes even if they do not want them.

Our view is that participation, with clear limits, should benefit rather than hinder this work because it should lead to a higher quality of information and lessen the likelihood of the user resisting a course of action. But user participation in protective work may worry workers who feel that encouraging participation may obstruct the pursuit of protection. Certainly the law provides for social workers to impose some elements of investigation or assessment on individuals unwilling to be involved; but a participative stance will help in this, as it should clarify when such powers under the law are needed, and individuals should be able to understand more clearly the extent and limits of intrusion into their lives.

In our view, social work needs new words and concepts for the three stages of contact and new participative practices that will aid understanding, having a say, and accessible judgement. A user-oriented service would be less concerned with terms like investigation, assessment and review and more concerned with getting into the system, deciding on services at the start, and deciding on services in the light of user experience. It would also move away from the idea that users are passive and workers active, and move towards the idea that workers and users are both active. It would advance the role of workers as consultants to the user or, in protective services, as servants of the court.[17]

Social work should also facilitate public understanding of services. People often find services difficult to understand. There are technical terms, official forms, and different staff are in charge of different parts of the system. Inevitably people new to a system will not understand much about the process and they will worry about the impact of actions that they do or do not take.

Understanding a service is not an end in itself. People need enough understanding to be able to have their say. They should not be burdened with too much information, but they should understand the key elements necessary to participation. They should not be patronised, the information should be freely available, it should be appropriate to the stage of service that they are in, and it should be accessible within the users' own language and culture.

In order to be able to have your say, both confidence and knowledge are required. It is necessary to know the key points that should be addressed to influence outcome and to feel confident enough to make those points. The key points, people and meetings should be explained to the user in the information made available, and this should be accompanied by a style of service that, as far as possible, puts people at their ease, positively assists them in presenting their views, and is characterised by polite, pleasant and respectful behaviour of staff.

Last, people should have access to the criteria on which judgements by service providers are made. Records of contact, agreements for service, timetables for decisions, criteria for service allocation and respect for the user's experience of the service will all play a role in establishing people's knowledge of decision-making and opening up judgements to scrutiny. A policy of shared recording should be adopted with the worker completing most records in the user's presence. This is an active policy of user participation not a passive model of access being made available to records. Agreements for specific elements of service should be clearly made between user and worker and should always be put in writing. At the stage of entry into the system specific dates should be given for when decisions will be made. At the stage of service allocation clear criteria should be available for giving or withholding services, and options for other services should be covered. Finally, at the stage of review of service, increased weight should be given to users' views based on their direct experience of the service.

Proposals in relation to people's rights to participation

(1) People should have the right to expect social services to provide and work to a policy statement that commits the organisation to active user participation. There should be a clear indication that all stages of decision-making will be on the basis of a collaboration between user and worker. This policy should be widely publicised and available in attractive and accessible format and appropriate languages in all parts of the organisation that have public access.

(2) People should have the right to expect social services to define the limits that protective work will impose on taking users' views into account, and to define the ways in which users in these circumstances can limit intrusion into their lives.

(3) People should have the right to have information given to them as a matter of course, and not just on request. It should be given in a variety of ways including personal discussion and a range of documents.

(4) People should have the right to information which is clearly designed to encourage and enable users to have their say – it should emphasise the commitment of the agency to participation in its content and its design and in where it is available (for example information about child-care services should be provided in children's clinics, schools and perhaps in some local supermarkets).

(5) People should have the right to information which is simple and clear, and which avoids (or where they are necessary explains) professional terms. It should be relevant to each of the three stages of service: entry, beginning services or continuing services. The key points which a user needs to know in order to play an active role in the process should be highlighted.

(6) People should have the right to information in a form which is acceptable and accessible to the range of cultures and religions within the agency's catchment area (it should not just be tailored to those who currently use the service). Language and presentation and style should be appropriate.

(7) People should have the right to know the name of one individual who is responsible for their service. This person should be the contact point for the user and should always be prepared to accept responsibility for dealing with enquiries from the user. A back-up should be provided if this person is unavailable. The name of the manager of the service should be prominently displayed in public areas such as waiting rooms, with a brief and clear statement that this individual carries final responsibility for the quality of the service, and welcomes users' views.

(8) People should have the right to see any reports prepared about them and they should be able to indicate areas of positive agreement or disagreement with those

reports. They should have facilities to prepare their own reports including access to typing services and advice as to how to present their views.

(9) People should have the right to create jointly the records used in decision-making and there should be a clear and publicised policy about users' access to any third-party records which are received by the agency.

(10) People should have the right to publicised standards for key decisions (for example the length of time it will take to respond to a request for a home visit) and to a written explanation, with a copy to the director of social services, if these standards are not adhered to.

(11) People should have the right to expect that their evaluation of service will be regarded as an important element in future service planning.

Policy conclusions

The practice of social work involves the use of a great deal of professional discretion. Social workers normally provide individualised services based on professional judgements of need rather than standardised services. It would be impossible to formulate a complex specification of needs and rights to cover every individual circumstance that social workers might encounter. Nor could workers respond flexibly to individual problems if they were bound by rigid rules. Furthermore, social work operates on behalf of people who often have little social power. Thus, this extensive use of professional discretion poses special problems for a rights-based approach to welfare as it can be difficult for users to understand, influence and, if necessary, challenge professional decisions. Where people are compelled to receive a service, as in much child protection work, it is all the more important for the standards on which professional discretion is founded to be transparent to the user and open to question.

Professional judgements are not, of course, made in a vacuum. They are founded on social-work theories, the 'practice wisdom' accumulated during the course of professional experience, the prevailing office and agency culture, the legislative framework of social work, the policies and procedures of their agency and knowledge of available resources. At the very least, it should be possible to make the policies and procedures of the agency and, where appropriate, the relevant legislation, available to users of social services. This in itself would make the exercise of professional discretion less opaque. While this could not guarantee users a greater degree of participation in decision-making, it would at least create conditions in which it would be easier for users to understand and influence decision-making and, if necessary, to question professional decisions.

There are two broad strategies that social services departments could adopt in order to establish the rights outlined in this chapter. First, each agency should have an information policy requiring it to provide clear, well-presented influence decision-making and, if necessary, to question professional decisions.

There are two broad strategies that social services departments could adopt in order to establish the rights outlined in this chapter. First, each agency should have an information policy requiring it to provide clear, well-presented and accessible information in a variety of formats and languages. Information would be available about:

* policies and priorities;
* services available;
* criteria of eligibility for these services;
* who to contact to request a service;
* procedures for complaint, appeal and redress.

This information would help service users understand how professional discretion operates within a social services department. Information relevant to their particular circumstances would assist them in becoming involved in decision-making alongside professionals and in making their own choices wherever possible.

Second, users' rights to participate in defining their needs, negotiating agreements and making decisions should be backed by a publicly available set of procedural guidelines. Again, these should be clearly and imaginatively presented in a range of formats. These would aim to make the process of professional decision-making clearer and open to question. Such procedural guidelines could:

* explain the agency's assessment procedures (for child abuse investigations, community care assessments or other services);
* explain how decisions are made, by whom and how service users can ensure their own views are heard;
* outline service users' right to information relevant to their own case (to know the facts being considered, to have access to agency records and reports about them, and to participate in any case conferences or reviews);
* give users the right to a written account of the decisions taken (preferably in the form of an agreement negotiated with them), including the grounds for refusing service if appropriate, and how to appeal against the decision if necessary;
* in certain, specified cases give users the right to appoint an advocate to assist them in putting their case to a social services department (a provision of the Disabled Persons Act 1986 which has not been implemented).

These procedural guidelines would help to establish the rights we have outlined in this paper and would be particularly important in giving some protection to involuntary users of social services. Service users should be involved in drawing up these guidelines, through consultation with local user groups (such as the

National Association for Young People in Care and carers groups). This would help to ensure that the criteria for good practice embodied in guidelines are both relevant and empowering to users.

The status of such guidelines needs careful attention. Local codes of practice could be introduced, but without statutory back-up they may not be given high priority by agency staff and it would be difficult for users to ensure that they were enforced. One option would be the production of national guidance specifying the areas that each department's policy on procedural rights should address. This would be introduced either through legislation or in the form of a Department of Health circular. Such national guidance would require that the rights of service users associated with any particular procedure (such as the rights of parents and children in child-abuse investigations) should be clearly specified so that any failure to uphold these rights could provide an explicit basis for complaint and redress. This official guidance would serve as a framework for local negotiation.

At the national level, a further safeguard of the rights of users of social services would be the establishment of a general social services council,[18] as supported by a wide range of social-services organisations including the Association of the Directors of Social Services and the National Institute for Social Work. Among the jobs of this council should be the setting of standards of knowledge and competence the public may expect of a social worker. The existence of published standards would provide users with a yardstick against which to assess their personal experience. The process of setting standards would have to explore professional consensus about what is within the remit of individual social workers and what is possible only with the active collaboration and commitment of social-services authorities. We suggest the principles set out in this paper provide the basis for a serious debate within social work on the rights of its users.

7 REALISING RIGHTS THROUGH LOCAL SERVICE CONTRACTS

Wendy Thomson

In the early 1990s three political parties developed their own 'Citizens' Charters'. At the same time, the concept of citizenry and a national constitutional framework has been discussed as a basis for extending rights. Meanwhile, local authorities up and down the country have been developing practical methods for empowering local people. This chapter is primarily concerned with the third of these political processes.

I will describe how local authorities are developing new forms of governing and providing services to their communities. These initiatives all recognise that local democracy must mean more for more people if it is going to thrive. They mark an attempt to improve upon past practices, which gave individuals few opportunities to be involved in defining, organising or evaluating public services. They acknowledge that this lack of involvement has made people lose confidence in public services.

Local authorities and rights

The process by which local authorities have worked to empower their residents differs in important ways from that advocated by national political parties in their different Citizen's Charters, and by those arguing for social and economic rights to be inscribed in law.

First, local authorities operate without the power to pass legislation. The rules of 'ultra vires' allow them to act only where national legislation permits them to do so. They cannot simply rely on legislation to create rights but have to involve people in making them real. We can see one example of how this has worked in their experience of promoting race and sex equality.

In the 1970s, national concern with equal rights led to legislation which makes unfair discrimination on grounds of race or sex unlawful. The Commission for Racial Equality and the Equal Opportunities Commission were established to enforce legislation and to protect women and racial groups from discrimination. In the 1980s, many local authorities took up the cause of equal opportunities. Without legislative power, they instituted a range of practices aimed at eliminating discrimination in their employment practices and service delivery. By the 1990s, in spite of financial and legal restrictions imposed by central government, many authorities can show that they have changed the composition of their workforce – so that they are no longer dominated by older white men, but instead more closely reflect their diverse communities.

In employment and service delivery, race and sex discrimination operate by complex and often indirect means. These have been challenged not simply through litigation, but by changing the way services are organised and run: hours of opening, creches, translation and interpretation, use of plain language, public consultation, grant aiding a variety of organisations to provide services for the community, and so on. The equal rights legislation has played only a minor part in these changes. At times the law has been used to prevent change – for example by banning positive action and contract compliance. Mostly, though, the law simply hasn't been relevant.

Second, local authorities have demonstrated that change can be brought about not only in the absence of legislation, but also at a time when equality is not a priority for central government. This is an important minority right – localities should be able to pursue political priorities and programmes which are locally and democratically determined. This right of a locality can be enriched through local democratic structures, but without safeguards it can be even further eroded by national legislation. A centrally determined set of rights to specific economic and social benefits could seriously undermine the rights of local communities to govern themselves.

Third, local authorities have the sort of decentralised and representative structures that allow them to involve local people directly. Many of the services which they provide require direct interaction with people. In the last decade, some local authorities have taken decentralisation further then ever before. This move has had a number of objectives: to differentiate between areas and between people in areas; to make services more accessible geographically and more responsive to people's needs and preferences; to devolve power over the nature and organisation of local services. But however far down the decentralising road they go, all local authorities have a capacity to relate directly to citizens and to involve them in decision-making – a capacity not shared by central government.

Fourth, rather than relying on legislation to define in abstract terms universal social and economic rights, these local practices have directly involved people in highly differentiated standards of services, and means of ensuring their delivery. Their practice demonstrates that local authorities can provide people with the right to a say in the way their communities are governed and services are organised. Through local political processes, people are empowered by developing a capacity to influence the course of events. Any legislation which gives standard social rights must also give the right to be involved in determining what those rights will be and how they should be realised.

Equity, difference and local democracy

In theoretical discussions we can easily make false assumptions about who people are, what they want, and the extent to which they can exercise the means to secure what they want. It is easy to slip into a world where everyone is the same able self-advocate, with a framework of rights serving as a regulator to sets of relations between citizens and state. Real life is not like that.

No movement concerned about equal rights can afford to ignore the differences between citizens and how these differences are structured into inequality. For example, people's different relationships to the labour market will determine whether or not they have a job, its pay and security, income during illness or retirement, etc. If such important differences are ignored, equal rights can reproduce the inequality which welfare seeks to redress and citizenship is meant to overcome.

If a welfare system fails to meet people's needs, this does not stem solely from a lack of sufficient entitlements to goods and services. No less important is how decisions are made about what those entitlements will be and how people obtain them. No set of rights and entitlements will enhance people's welfare unless experts' ideas are challenged and people are brought into the process of defining and securing 'their own good'.

Any national programme which contains a drive for democracy needs to allow different priorities and outcomes to be expressed in different areas. Once people's differences and the implications for local services are recognised, the job of representing and serving the public is changed. It is not a question of delivering standard sets of services in sufficient quantities to those most in need. To provide relevant and responsive services means understanding people's diverse needs as they fragment, polarise and change. This movement and diversity has to be addressed democratically in order for public services to be appropriate and for the public sphere which nourishes them to flourish.

One danger implied in the discourse on rights – as the social and economic goods of citizenship – is the assumption that a universal citizenship exists with common interests.[1] This view assumes that all or particular groups of citizens (distinguished by race, sex or class, for example) have interests which are predetermined and homogeneously shared. Many political movements have mistakenly believed this to be the case. As a result they overlook their own role in constructing those interests and organising the capacity to meet them.

If public services carry a monolithic image of the public – whether it be that of a male industrial worker, an estate agent, journalist or a slightly desperate single mum – they will not contain a capacity to deal with people's different requirements. That failure will compound existing inequalities. To create real opportunity for all people, public services need to involve a variety of individuals and groups, and must develop forms of organisation that encourage this involvement.

One strategy for encouraging local involvement is decentralisation. In the London borough of Islington, for example, housing, social and environmental services have been devolved to 24 locations, where they are provided from one office responsible for a neighbourhood. In other authorities, single functions such as housing or social services are being devolved. Smaller organisations based in neighbourhoods are likely to be easier to access and influence. It thus becomes more difficult for employees and managers to carry on with mistaken ideas about the public, or the public about the service.

This also implies moving away from traditional professionalism, where the experts believe they know it all, to a more open and interactive setup, where professionals recognise the need to learn from those they serve. Moreover, as different professionals are brought closer to each other as well as to the community, it becomes more difficult to 'clientise' citizens into narrow definitions of need and treatment. As full people, rather than people with fragmented 'needs' or problems, residents have a better chance of becoming active citizens in their neighbourhoods, its services and public life.

In some authorities, neighbourhood forums, tenants' associations, and other such groups are becoming active not only as users of services, or pressure groups lobbying in their particular interests; they are taking part in the governing of their communities and its services, in partnership with local authority politicians and staff.

In these circumstances, the scope for improving the effectiveness of the services soars. But it does so only if residents play an active part and become the 'subjects', not passive objects, of service delivery.

Public responsibility

It is no longer enough, if it ever was, to concentrate on maximising the volume of standard services or cutting costs. What counts is not just how many of the local population should get which service, but the range and quality of services.

The task of local authorities is different from that faced by the private service or retail sector. Few people can afford to do most of their weekly shop at Marks and Spencer – the range and quality may be there, but so is the cost, passed on in the price. The price serves to distribute as well as to finance the goods and services which Marks and Spencer sell. They pitch their market to get the kind of trade-off between price and quality that makes good business sense.

The power most consumers experience is not to shop at Marks and Spencers very often. Those who cannot afford a regular diet of quality goods at M&S prices 'choose' to do without, or to find cheaper alternatives. It matters not to Marks and Spencer.

Local authorities by contrast have a social responsibility to be concerned about the consequences of both providing and not providing services. This distinction will remain, regardless of how the current debate about 'contracting out' is resolved. If the public is paying collectively, and issues of distribution and access are to be determined on the basis of citizenship rather than price, then the key question to be addressed is not how services can be 'sold' to the public, but how decisions about distribution and access can be taken democratically.

Public services are not in the business of pitching for a market. Often, they have to provide universal services – where the aim is to make sure that everyone gets something. Often, they have to ration scarce resources. The decisions are highly political and require a robust democracy. Yet some local authorities have spent the 1980s disengaging from the public, as they have sought to solve problems by selling off or contracting out services. Those who have moved in the opposite direction, seeking to solve problems by getting closer to local communities and engaging in direct dialogue with them, may be better equipped to meet the challenges of the 1990s.

From this perspective local government is not just about delivering services but also about enriching local democracy; the two are inextricable linked. Here, the weaknesses of political culture in British society present a serious practical problem. People need to understand that the organisation and outcomes of public policy can improve only if they themselves are part of that process. Unless this happens, 'rights' – whether for citizens or customers – are only useful for those who can afford lawyers.

The day-to-day experience of relating to democratically run local services is a world with which many central government politicians and civil servants are unfamiliar. It is messy and frightening for technocrats. Its outcomes cannot easily be reduced to figures on the accountant's balance sheet which so dominated local politics in the 1980s. There are now signs that the public is rebelling against the reduction of all public and social life to the cash nexus. If services are to be assessed in terms of quality and not just cash, people have to be involved in that assessment. Neither the quality of the expert nor the standards of the assembly line will satisfy. Local 'Citizens' Charters', complaints procedures, service contracts, service sampling, training for staff and management, and quality audits: these are some of the processes through which local authorities are involving their residents in securing more effective government and services for their communities.[2]

But it is the idea of service contracts that has attracted most attention.

The next part of this chapter will describe some local authority service contracts, the services chosen, how they have gone about it, and the outcomes so far.

Service contracts in practice

Underlying service contracts, or public service agreements, is a simple idea but a complex political reality. For services to be accountable to the people who vote and pay for them, residents need to be clear what they can expect, and what they can do if those expectations are not met. The 'agreement' establishes a set of guarantees, together with reciprocal responsibilities. The agreement sets out procedures to be followed if what is guaranteed is not delivered.

The form and content of a contract are almost infinitely variable, depending on the service itself, the locality, the resources available and what local people want. Broadly, they can change the way local people experience services in a range of ways, including:

* * having a say in deciding about services for their community;
* * choosing between different services or providers;
* * being treated with courtesy and respect;
* * knowing the services and the standards they can expect;
* * having a say in judging the quality of services;
* * being clear about their public responsibility;
* * having a right to redress.

Several local authorities including York, Milton Keynes, Basildon, Leicester, Cardiff, Darlington, Harlow, North Tyneside, Oxford, Rochdale, Newcastle, Islington, Lewisham and Merton have introduced contracts with their citizens for such services as refuse collection, street sweeping, swimming pools and housing repairs. These have been locally generated to meet specific experiences. They have not been instigated as part of any detailed national plan. Steps are being taken to introduce service contracts into more personal services, such as community care, education and child protection.

In the next section, I describe the process of establishing service contracts, drawing on the experience, to date, of several local authorities. I show how the process differs for different kinds of service – depending on whether they are universal, such as refuse collection; quasi-market, such as swimming pools; or rationed, such as council housing. I then discuss extending the idea of service contracts to personal welfare services, particularly community care and child protection. The term 'contract' is used here generically, to cover undertakings that may be called 'contracts', 'agreements' or 'guarantees'; it is not intended to imply that this is the only term being used or to suggest that they are legally binding. That remains to be seen.

A universal service: refuse collection and street sweeping

So far, the services which have most frequently been subject to service contracts have been those provided on a universal basis. Refuse collection was selected for several reasons. Everyone relies on it, but they do not take an active part in using it until something goes wrong. The contract offers an opportunity to do something to put it right. The service is relatively simple and more readily subject to specification than other services. Another reason is that it has been comprehensively specified in preparation for compulsory competitive tendering in many authorities. Most critically for selecting any service for a contract, it has to be working. And it has to be perceived as working not only by elected members, managers, and employees, but also by the public.

Furthermore, while there is no natural coincidence of views about the purpose and standards of service between the public, workforce, managers and elected representatives, refuse collection enjoys more consensus than most. The first step in the process of establishing a service contract is agreeing the nature and standard of the service people want and can expect. The wider the consensus about what the service is, the more effective the contract will be experienced by the public.

Finding out what people want

Even in refuse collection, we found that there are different expectations in different social groups and localities. For example, opinion surveys show that leafier neighbourhoods, already objectively cleaner than others, are often less satisfied with the standard and performance of the service. Opinion surveys of this kind, which are often a useful first step in the process of agreeing the specification for a service, show that political decisions remain important. Consumer research can improve the understanding on which political decisions are based, and contribute to any assessment of whether the service is working.

In Islington's 24 neighbourhoods, the specification for the refuse collection was discussed with neighbourhood forums, traders, business, and local amenity groups. Managers from the cleansing department went out to meetings with groups in the community, where they presented information about resources and possible options for consideration, as well as questions designed to elicit views. The specification was drawn up in the light of these discussions; it was then put out to tender, the contract awarded, and the specification inscribed in a local service contract with residents.

Within the parameters of legislation, council policy and finance, residents could express some choice. For example, they said they wanted the refuse collected from the front door rather than from the curbside, and from inside the homes of people with disabilities. They made helpful suggestions for improving the co-ordination of refuse and street-sweeping rotas. They ensured that the number of bins allocated took account of family size and lifestyle. Some residents' preferences were blocked by legislation: for example, the Conservative Government's ban on contract compliance meant they could not be guaranteed a workforce which reflected the community.

It is clear that even this fairly standard service had previously been experienced unequally by some groups in the community. This may seem a relatively minor form of discrimination, but it illustrates a more serious point about the unintended consequences of standard service entitlements, even for a relatively straightforward service such as refuse collection. It is possible to customise the service to accommodate some of the differences between different households, but this must be done at a very local level.

Specifying the service

Service contracts for refuse collection can be based on consultation that results in a publicly agreed specification. Some aspects are primarily a matter for the authority's contract with service providers – issues like work rotas, cost, penalties, and organisational capacity. Others are a matter for residents. The authority's contract with them includes the time and day of collection, quality features like closing gates, replacing bin lids and clearing spillage, and the right to redress if the service does not live up to the standard publicised.

Contracts tend to cover one area at a time and can represent a guarantee to the local community as well as to the individuals who live there. Residents can be involved through the neighbourhood forums in vetting the contract before it is distributed and their knowledge can help to ensure that the specification which appears on paper is reflected in the service received on the doorstep. Information needs to be accurate and clear. At a neighbourhood level it is possible to inform residents precisely when their refuse will be collected and from where, exactly how to have bulky items and garden refuse taken away, and to whom and where to address compliments or complaints.

One way of publicising the contract is through a leaflet which clearly states the terms of the agreement, along with instructions about what to do if the terms are not met. Other forms of publicity can be used – advertisements in local papers or radio, posters, black and minority ethnic media as well as community networks.

What if the service doesn't work?

The national media, in investigating these local service contracts, have shown close interest in whether or not they are legally enforceable or backed up by financial compensation. In fact, most local authorities have found that this is not residents' main concern. In theory, they can now sue councils for a whole range of things, from cracked pavements to unlawful quantities of specified litter on strictly categorised roads, but this rarely gives them what they most need – which is for their local services to work.

The manner of compensation when services fall below their guarantee needs to be adapted to the service and to the circumstances. In refuse collection, a service which is free at the point of delivery, many people would rather have their bins emptied than receive a small cash penalty when they are not.

Introducing cash into individuals' relationships with local authorities is something that should not be undertaken lightly (as the problems arising from the Poll Tax demonstrate). Some services are already bought and paid for at the point of delivery, and have a billing and cash collection capacity. A service such as domestic refuse collection does not. Implementing a system of financial penalties requires a centralised administration. When it was suggested in some localities during discussions about a service contract, residents argued against it. They were concerned that a system of cash penalties could be abused and didn't feel it justified the cost of setting up a regulatory system to investigate and verify claims. And still a cash payment would not get the refuse collected quickly.

Assessing and publicising the result

Residents have a right to know how the service contract is working. Although it is still too early to give a picture in most authorities, the intention is to publish reports regularly about how the service performed against the standards publicly agreed. Feedback from the public – through individual enquiries or complaints, as well as user surveys – will form important sources of information for this assessment.

Most authorities experience fewer public complaints than they feared they might, but usually more than they would have in the days before service contracts. An increase in complaints can be anticipated following the implementation of service contracts, for several reasons. The service is being given a high public profile, it is communicating widely its standards, and the process of making contact with the necessary council officer is being streamlined and encouraged.

People tend to complain if they have reason to believe it will make a difference – and this is to be encouraged. Refuse collection makes an interesting comparison with the poll tax, for example, which is highly unpopular, but elicits far fewer complaints. It may be that people feel there is nothing anyone can do about putting it right. Another change is that the 'quality' of complaints seems to improve. By this I mean that people's complaints are better informed by a clear expectation of what the service was supposed to provide. They are more likely to be confident in claiming their right to it, and able to be more precise about where it needs to improve.

A quasi-market service: swimming pools

A swimming-pool service involves choice. No one has to use swimming pools, and in some localities there may be private as well as public provision. Consumer preferences can be powerful factors in determining the nature of the service and the standards it should meet.

The process of negotiating the terms of a service contract informs managers and politicians of what matters to users and residents. In an optional service, there are often differences of opinion between those who use it and those who do not. Negotiations prior to an agreement or contract can help find out what the public generally and users specifically think is a reasonable standard of service. It can also help to reconcile differences between them.

As far as swimming pools are concerned, what matters to people in some areas is that the pools should be open as publicised, that the water temperature is comfortable, that water and changing rooms are clean, and that there are appropriate rules and sufficient supervision to make the pools safe.

The process of negotiation is similar to that for a universal service, but because it is optional, there are some differences. In addition to discussing terms with neighbourhood forums and other community groups to get the general view, users themselves need to be consulted. This can be done, for example, by inviting users to join small discussion groups as they enter or leave the pool, or by issuing questionnaires to users, or both. Where users' and non-users' views conflict, the differences between them can be discussed further locally, or elected councillors may need to decide. There is no hard-and-fast formula, and the process is bound to be messy and unsatisfying for some. But as long as it remains open and adaptable, and contains a practical process for reaching a decision, it can serve its purpose – which is to reach an agreement in a way that is likely to be widely supported, of what is to be provided for whom, and what to do when things go wrong.

This must include an understanding of how the service is targeted: it isn't just a matter of who can pay, but who should benefit from the service. That means deciding how to allocate subsidies (free, low-price and full-price admissions), and how to organise sessions throughout the day and week, to ensure that different needs are met. Within this policy framework, a service contract can guarantee that people who are using the service, however they have been attracted by programming and pricing, are receiving what they have been promised.

Extending guarantees presents different issues which need to be resolved for each service. In swimming pools, methods must be found of establishing standards of water cleanliness. In one locality, pool users were concerned about the potentially harmful effects of both bacteria and the chemicals employed to control them. When experts were consulted about how to set up a publicly accountable system, they suggested a fearfully complex method. It involved publishing a technical specification for safe levels of bacteria and chemicals, arranging systems by which people could access free water testing in public laboratories, and putting the public's test results against the evidence of those running the pools.

Through discussions with users and pools staff, it became clear that there was little enthusiasm for a system of this kind. Most people seemed to be satisfied if they could see their feet at the bottom of the pool and there was no floating debris – and this was what was eventually written into the service contract. In other localities, people might feel differently. But here again, a contract can be customised to meet residents' particular requirements, not only for cleanliness, but also for hours of opening, the scope of services, safety, and redress. In a feepaying service like pools, if agreed standards are not met, people who complain can get a voucher for a free swim.

Rationed services: housing

Some local authorities have introduced service contracts for housing repairs or other housing services. When the contract has included a wide range of rights for tenants, authorities have treated it as a Tenants' Charter. (These have been established in some local authorities long before the Conservative Government's Citizen Charter initiatives.) Similar principles and steps are involved. The guarantee is customised to cover the priorities and preferences negotiated with local tenants, sometimes differentiated by estate, neighbourhood or street. The contract specifies what a good service is, how it will be provided, and what redress there will be if it is not carried out.

That said, housing raises a particular set of issues which have to be addressed. For example, the logic of a housing repair service is based on the line drawn between private and public responsibility in the landlord/tenant relationship. Preparing a local service contract involves public discussion about where that line should be drawn, and the decision can then be made explicit. Choices can be made about what housing professionals call 'rechargeable' – i.e. the repairs which the landlord charges to the individual tenant, on the ground that the damage is considered to be the tenant's fault (replacing locks when tenants lose the keys, or clearing drains). Again, there is not a natural consensus among whole groups of tenants or even particular estates about what should be tenants' responsibility in such matters. But through discussion and in circumstances where choices involve real consequences, it is possible for a view to be reached.

When there are choices to be made – between speed of response, cost and quality, rent levels and special amenities, voids, repair and redecoration – there is more chance of getting the balance right for citizens if tenants are actively involved in constructing that balance and monitoring its practical application.

Housing repair services have a high profile and are often problematic in local authorities with large housing stocks. Building works departments have been in the forefront of the Conservative Government's policies of privatisation. But not all authorities have seen this as the best solution. There are not always private firms willing or able to take on the necessary scale and range of work at a reasonable price and rate of response. And the track record of private firms is as varied in quality and price as those in the public sector.

Some authorities have tried to empower tenants through democratic means rather than relying simply on market mechanisms – for example, by setting up housing co-operatives or tenant management agreements. Many authorities have also decentralised their housing management. Whatever kind of collective arrangements are made, however, service contracts for housing repairs provide guaranteed standards of repair, within fixed time frames. Some provide last-resort options for tenants to employ directly an alternative builder to undertake the repair as a form of redress if the terms are not met by the authority's contractor. There is, at least, an established private market in this field, even though generally the sector is regarded no more highly by most customers, and dealt with guardedly. Nevertheless, this option exists for individual housing repairs in a way that is not possible in other services.

Service contracts give tenants a right to repair beyond the statutory rights which currently exist. The Landlord and Tenant Act 1985 (Section 11) offers a civil remedy for breach of landlord duty regarding repairs to the tenant's property. It places a burden on landlords to maintain the structure and exterior of the premises and the water, gas, sanitation and electricity installations. This provision is used mostly against private landlords and obliges them to do repairs once they are notified of the need by the court. Another legal remedy is the Environmental Protection Act 1990 (Section 82) which refers to nuisance caused to an individual and is heard in the Magistrates Court under criminal proceedings. It requires tenants to notify the landlord (public or private) of their complaint and their intention to bring proceedings. An action can require the landlord to execute repairs to prevent the nuisance. Under both Acts the court can order compensation to the tenant.

These legal proceedings require the tenant to engage a lawyer. Proceedings are inherently antagonistic, and can involve a lengthy, costly procedure. Most people do not think the law provides an effective solution for the 'right to repair'. A service contract is different in that its terms are negotiated and agreed by both parties. It can be geared to local conditions and to the preferences of relatively small groups of people. It involves the commitment of the landlord to agreed forms of redress. These can be set in motion relatively quickly and without recourse to law. It is more likely to be accessible to tenants and less likely to expose them to the risk of losing reasonable claims.

Far more is asked of social landlords than of those in the private rented sector. There, the landlord is satisfied if a flat is occupied and the rent paid; the tenant is happy if tenure is secure and conditions stable; there is no wider expectation that public interest be served. In the social sector, however, rent and occupation are not the only indicators of performance. The community as a whole has an interest in ensuring that scarce housing resources are being properly used and maintained. An empty flat in the public sector means something different for residents than one in the private sector; an occupied flat is considered a benefit only if occupied by the tenant rightfully entitled to it under a democratically agreed allocations policy.

Repairs are just one of many services which can be built into a local Tenants' Charter – which becomes in effect a more elaborate and comprehensive service contract. A Tenants' Charter can be drawn up for a whole area or for an individual estate or group of homes. In addition to housing repairs, it will make explicit rent levels, the frequency and form of payment, additional amenities and rental supplements, estate-management services, caretaking, ground mainten-ance, emergency services, telephone numbers and contact points. Local charters can express the priorities of different areas; they can rely on existing local institutions to carry out the terms of the agreement, with the involvement of tenants' associations. The local authority can help to ensure that common standards of equity and economy are shared where these are considered important to the wider community.

Can service contracts work in other types of services?

The question I shall now address is whether service contracts can be extended to personal social services – in particular, to community-care services for people affected by ageing, disability and mental or physical illness, and to child protection.

There are at least two reasons why they should be. First, few public services have been more criticised than personal social services and their professional workforce. So much so that social workers often lack the personal or public confidence and authority which a profession needs to work effectively. Bombarded by scandals and caught in the crossfire of a political conflict about the nature and purpose of public welfare, social workers have few supporters. From this position it will not be easy to construct a contract that will be taken seriously by the public. They need to improve their credibility. A first step would be to come out of their isolation and engage directly with the public in discussions about what they do, with whom and why. This might help find ways to involve the public in the social responsibilities which social workers are attempting to deal with on their own.

Second, personal social services are experienced in individual and subjective terms. It is not helpful to speak of universal entitlements to standard services when this is the case. So it is important to involve people actively in agreeing what personal welfare is for them, and what help they want to achieve it.

The practical process of involving people in social services – for services to both adults and children – is ensuring them the right to have their needs assessed and taken into account. This is not the way services are organised at the moment and it will involve an important change for this to be brought about. However, some authorities are beginning to work in this way, and are introducing service contracts as part of the change.

Chapter 6, on social work, explores some of the main issues at stake here. What follows is concerned more particularly with how the mechanism of service contracts can be used.

A personal service: community care

The NHS and Community Care Act 1990 introduces a framework intended to enable people affected by ageing or disability to remain living at home. There is considerable scepticism about the financial motives underlying this legislation, and even greater pessimism about health and local authorities having the resources that are required to meet the expectations it implies. Nevertheless, some authorities consider that the opportunities created by the Act nationally provide scope for extending the rights of service users and their carers.

The Act places a duty upon local authorities to assess the whole community's need for community services annually through a community care plan. It also requires authorities to carry out an assessment of individual adults and their need for support. Whatever the Government's intentions, both these requirements – planning for the needs of the community and assessing the needs of individuals – may be used to strengthen user's rights by ensuring them a say in their care and their community. The two are linked: individual assessments provide the knowledge and means by which, over time, the community care plan becomes better informed.

If the model of assessment is needs-oriented, the wishes of service users and carers are central and put in the context of their community. Its goal would be the identification of a range of appropriate support rather than standard pre-fixed services. People who carry out such assessments would need to act as advocates for their clients. The idea is that the range and quality of services available in the community will change in response to people's expressed needs.

This approach would be different from assessing whether or not someone qualifies for particular services. In order to ration scarce resources, services have often had to contain limits which have little to do with what people need and which it is difficult for them to do anything to change. For example, some home care services will undertake one set of tasks but not another, during only one part of the day or night, for individuals in one set of circumstances, thereby excluding others. Moreover, access to social care may be less crucial in determining people's capacity to remain living in the community than access for people with disabilities and carers to mainstream public services such as transport, education, and housing.

The Community Care Act does not entitle every adult to an assessment. Rather, it requires authorities to publish their own criteria for determining who will be assessed. A service contract could guarantee individuals who are in particular circumstances a full assessment, within a set time limit. An example would be all pupils leaving special schooling, all people referred (by themselves or others) for particular services such as sheltered housing, a nursing home, or day care.

People in these circumstances could be guaranteed a certain standard of assessment through a service contract which involved:

* one main assessor to act as the point of contact and co-ordination;
* access to a range of specialists where necessary;
* user and carer having a say, with the right to express a different view;
* the outcome in a written statement formally recognising their needs and preferences;
* a fixed time limit, with a review in an agreed number of months.

Although they have no statutory duty to do so, most socially-minded authorities will want to arrange for care following the assessment. A service contract can extend to this second stage – and guarantee individuals a specific set of supports. With the state of many communities and their care resources, it would be impractical to offer people a blanket right to live in the community. Nor is it a right which everyone would find desirable. However, there could be a process of negotiation following the assessment, where individuals could agree with the authorities the help that they would actually receive. This process could lead to an individual plan for each person with their needs and the specific help they will receive clearly set out in a service contract.

The terms of such service contracts would need to take account of the personal, family and community circumstances of each individual. What people want in personal care services is flexibility and maximum personal control. Help might include a combination of community interventions – making housing or local facilities accessible, employment and training opportunities, community safety, transport, income security and financial advice, as well as traditional social care services such as respite and home care, general and specialist health services, meals, and so on.

This could mean a number of public service providers – from the NHS, social security, police, voluntary service organisations, as well as a number of local authority departments – entering into a set of commitments to an individual user and being held accountable for those commitments. Writings on public administration have long bemoaned the problems of coordination of the large departments of state. It would be truly a step forward for their services, within a politically determined policy, to be user-focused and directly accountable in a service contract to the people who rely upon them.

These service contracts would need to be regularly reviewed and updated. This again confronts some of the big problems experienced in social services – of people becoming clients and then being stuck at whatever level of functioning or help they were given when they first encountered the formal service system. Service contracts could automatically expire at a certain date, and have to be renewed to again come into effect. The terms could be changed to take account of an individuals' changed functioning or circumstances, or because they have changed their mind about the sort of help they thought they wanted.

Contracts open up ways of involving users directly in evaluating matters of professional competence. The traditional professional view is that personal social services are too personal and complex to be externally assessed. Some professional practices undertake spot audits of their casework, as a means of addressing the need for some evaluation. But service contracts could enable the individual user to contribute to the review process. Whatever professionals may rightfully feel about the complexity, knowledge and skill involved in their work, if the client feels a personal support service isn't working for them, then in an important sense it isn't working at all.

People will have differing abilities to participate actively in negotiating and exercising their rights under a service contract. Too often services treat everyone as if they were uniformly unable. Users relay their experiences of being told 'you must be confused dear' when they have complained that their home carer has not arrived at the appointed time, or they did not receive the meal they ordered. This is clearly not very empowering, and never justified. Nevertheless, for service contracts to work ways must be found of taking account of people's differing abilities to negotiate actively on their own behalf. No one is able to act independently in all respects, but help or advocacy needs to enable individuals to do so as they see fit. Social services and users' groups have considerable experience of this, and ideas about how it might be done, which can be built upon.

Care must be taken to ensure that where advocates are used, they do not undermine people's abilities by becoming another set of experts. It may not be a significant help to vulnerable people to have their interests fought over by two professionals with different but similarly unresponsive attitudes. One way of avoiding this might be to recruit advocates from a variety of people from different backgrounds, including people who themselves have an experience of disability. Advocates would need to act not only to assist with the negotiation of the service contract, but also to play a role in verifying whether or not it has been delivered as specified.

The question of redress is difficult when one considers the potential consequences of whether or not community care services are working well. In some extreme cases, the non-provision of the service may result in a fatal accident. At other times, it may be a matter of personal comfort or convenience. Here, too, it is unlikely that one form of redress could appropriately deal with the whole range of eventualities.

The idea of introducing service contracts at the point of assessment is being developed in some localities as a means of giving rights to service users and carers. The following set of principles underpins the approach which Islington is developing with the help of the King's Fund Centre:

(1) The right to be consulted and to have the opportunity to influence the pattern of support.

(2) Access to services which promote the greatest self-determination on the basis of well-informed and realistic choice.

(3) A right to support and participation in the community which does not exploit or disadvantage others.

(4) A right to use services which give the best chance of participation as valued members of the community, so services which are free of stigma.

(5) A right to culturally appropriate forms of community support, particularly for people from black and minority ethnic communities.

(6) A commitment to honest sharing of information about the resources available and the provision of service.

Turning these principles into practice will not come about through formal policy statements or the good intentions of professionals alone. To exist in practice, rights have to be advocated actively and realised in relationships between people with disabilities, carers and public services. This is where service contracts play a part.

The process so far has involved setting up on a neighbourhood basis new approaches to assessing the needs of individuals. Some of these processes build upon good practice which exists in parts of many authorities, but it takes on different priorities and perspectives when it happens outside the boundaries of individual services and involves a range of occupations from different agencies.

Discussing with users their experience of service with senior health and local authority managers has helped put the focus on what really counts. It is important that management is in touch with how clients perceive their performance in service terms. What has emerged from this process is that people want clear information, services flexible enough to adapt to their personal needs, one stop access, and certainty of provision once promised.

Consultation in the social services field is sometimes seen as too risky an undertaking, unless there is a lot of money to deal with the demands that will result. In fact, in this process people have been reasonable about their demands when they are fully in the picture. A realistic dialogue should be possible. After all, many people in these circumstances have considerable experience of not obtaining everything they want. The rights of people affected by ageing and disability are more often mediated by low expectations than impossible demands. Involving them is crucial.

In discussions with service users, the legal status of the assessment and service contract has not been their prime concern. What matters most is being able to live at home if they wish, regardless of the cost, or of the view of their families or professionals. It may not mean getting everything they want but it should mean receiving what they are promised. At home they wish to sustain a normal life, to choose the people who are going to care for them, and to be able to count on them to come when, and do what, they agreed. This needs to include evening and weekend caring and a social life integrated into that of their communities and social groups. If this does not happen, then they will want to be able to access some other means of help.

The practical possibilities for helping people to live in the community, and involving them in a right to that help through service contracts, will depend upon the resources and opportunities available in the localities where people live. One thing seems certain: there is little point in giving vulnerable people cash unless the care they want is actually available and accessible, at a price they can afford. Neither is a long legal battle much use as a means for compensating for damage to the quality of one's life. The whole point is to deliver some help that counts, and this should be the focus for the contract and system of redress.

The changes needed to shift public resources from institutional to community services are enormous. Nearly 30 years after the introduction of community care policy in mental health, current NHS spending is £1.4 billion. While £800 million supports some 40,000 in long-stay mental hospitals only £600 million supports more than 2 million people living in the community. In other words, £76 per day is spent on people in hospital compared with 29p. a day on people living in the community.[3] It will require a powerful force to effect the changes which users are advocating. Twenty years of national community care policy and top down 'priority group' planning, have not made a very substantial impact.

Consuming with little choice: child protection

The problem of power and legitimation for welfare services is particularly clear in child protection. Local authorities are facing choices about how they carry out the Children Act when public confidence in their ability to protect children, and respect parents, is at a low ebb. The risk is that social services will withdraw even further into the apparent protection of the isolated professional specialist. In these circumstances, elected members can feel tempted to leave the professionals to get on with it, living in hope that 'it won't happen here'.

Some professionals say that it is impossible to involve clients whose relationship with the authority is involuntary. They argue that if individuals could agree to a set of rights and responsibilities and behave accordingly, then the need for protection services would probably not exist. The very problem with many of these clients is that they cannot behave as they should or need to in order to fulfil social expectations of being a parent or young person. However, sooner or later the professional's ability to protect children and support families relies on obtaining their consent to change their behaviour.

If the process of preparing a contract involves the family or individual concerned in something akin to 'talks about talks', then it may provide a step toward a more effective child protection practice. An alternative is the surprise removal of the child, but this simply delays the moment when discussions must take place about why parents are not considered able to look after their child, what they have to do to demonstrate that they can, and how the authorities will help them.

The Children Act suggests the use of service agreements, alongside or instead of legal decisions about children's care or protection. One aim would be to use such agreements to develop active partnerships in protecting children, with explicit expectations for all sides – parents, children, and agencies. They could include people's right to be directly involved in decisions and to have a tangible avenue for redress. Organisations such as Family Rights Groups are working with some local authorities to extend parental participation to the assessment and review stage.

Some pointers from other experiences of introducing contracts might suggest how they would work in social services for children and families locally. The process of negotiating a service contract might begin with open discussion with the community about its expectations for its children, for themselves and their neighbours. In Britain there is confusion in many people's minds about what the family ought to mean. The family is officially regarded as a private matter – beyond the reaches of the state – and yet the state is often obliged to intervene in families, for sound reasons. Hence the need for public debate to reach a wider agreement about what should and should not be done by the collective in the family domain. Service contracts cannot fill the vacuum but they could provide a democratic means for clarifying the issues locally and setting the foundations for building public confidence in a children's service.

Through discussion of the general rights and responsibilities of a child protection service, the community can provide the reference point so badly needed to gauge the performance of social service policy and practice. These aims and standards cannot be taken as given and uncontested – the exclusive realm of the expert.

If a wider agreement could be constructed for the community's aims for its child protection service, then it would be possible to establish service contracts for individuals within this explicitly normative framework. Individual contracts 'customised' to the particular needs and circumstances of the child and parent(s) could help make explicit the aims of social intervention, strike an appropriate balance between care and control, construct a way to overcome conflicts between parental and children's rights, and set out mutual responsibilities, systems for their review and (where necessary) redress.

The Children Act provides parents and children with rights to representation and recourse to the courts. But everyone will not feel the same facility with the law, nor consider that judicial processes can serve their children's best interests. Some may prefer to follow an agreement voluntarily entered into with a local authority. Alternatively, detailed service contracts between parents, children, and other agencies could form part of the means of realising court decisions after they have been made.

Working with other agencies such as health authorities and police departments, local authorities may encounter different views about the idea of explicit agreements with 'patients' or 'perpetrators'. Their practical capacity to be open and specific about their services will need to be worked through, but there is much to be gained from engaging the public in matters of welfare and protection. Service agreements may provide one method for making this move.

Some organisational issues

Employees and users

Ensuring a voice for citizens and listening to what they say is a political job. Elected representatives have to take the lead in showing that interest and encouraging others to do the same. On this basis, and within a clear political framework, service providers have an important role to play. Employees, manual and professional, are in daily contact with service users. That contact at its best can be a fruitful dialogue and sow the seeds for a new partnership between service providers and users.

Most writing in public management argues that service providers are key – organisational statements espouse the importance of staff to delivering responsive and high-quality services. Programmes training staff in 'customer care' and quality management can be found on the agenda of many local authorities. Management, communications and training are central to all these initiatives – and we are counting the cost of under-investing in them in the past. Even John Major's initial tough talk about docking pay and instituting penalties prior to launching his Citizen's Charter, has given way to talk of positive incentives.

But in public sector employee relations there are different as well as common interests between the providers and users of service. In the past the balance too often may have tipped towards the interests of providers. Certainly providers are well placed to advance their interests, compared with the position in which most users find themselves. Consider the detailed protection for professionals and workforce contained in codes of practice and trade-union agreements. When staff become anxious about the implications for their rights of service contracts, they need to consider this – and ask whether the protection they enjoy may at times impede their ability to serve the public as responsively and flexibly as they might wish. Bureaucratic procedures can imprison as well as protect.

In empowering users we need to be aware that it is not simply the external mechanisms of organisation or statutory rights that protect people from getting short shrift. Individuals need to believe in their personal power to voice their needs and have their rights respected. You can't empower people without their agency – and what is critical here is the detail of personal interaction between individual users and individual providers. Professional and trade union traditions do not always recognise the importance of this agency, either in their members or in consumers. To be relevant to the public services of the 1990s they will need to do so.

Scope and limitations of service contracts

The practice of introducing service contracts is at an early stage. It is being developed from the priorities and requirements of different localities. It is not possible even if it were desirable, to provide a blueprint of how such agreements should work in every area for every service. Nor is it possible at this stage thoroughly to evaluate their success in empowering citizens in their relationships with local authority services.

What can be seen in the localities where service contracts have been introduced, is that they seem to provide some benefits. They appear to be popular with residents who are glad to have a say in planning the service and an honest statement of what they can expect. With that clear expectation they feel able to make representation through complaints or other means, to obtain the service as promised.

In addition to these benefits from the users' point of view, there is a whole range of managerial benefits which should improve the efficiency and effectiveness of the service. Service contracts provide a direct circle of accountability between the elected members, management, staff, and public/user – and back again. This can harness an enormous organisation in the single-minded pursuit of policy-directed, user-oriented service. This is likely to be a far more powerful force than procedural guidance cascading through bureaucratic hierarchies, or adding more costly supervisory layers. It has proved to be more meaningful than the simulations of profits and competition found in compulsory tendering requirements, or the paper consumer relationships on which internal markets rely.

However, there are limits too. Service contracts could become meaningless as they become more common and extend to many services. Like any currency, to have value, contracts need to represent meaningful entitlements, in which people have a personal interest and investment. In purely personal and practical terms there is a limit to how many individual contracts people will want.

Service contracts are only one of a variety of methods of empowerment. They may strengthen residents' expectations of universal services, like refuse collection or street sweeping. Or they may emulate market choice and value in a subsidised optional service like swimming pools. In a service like council housing where scarcity and rationing are key aspects of the contemporary relationship, then service contracts may give tenants some rights even when the right to choose is not one they can really afford to exercise. When centred on more personal relationships – for example in supporting community living, or setting out rights of parents in their child's protection – such contracts may become an important promise of public support necessary for personal survival.

The method needs to be centred on the user's perspective – to bring together the sometimes fragmentary welfare provision emanating from various departments, professions and statutes. No charter emanating from the heights of national government or inscribed in legislation is likely to deliver that 'seamless personal service' on the ground. The reality is that departments of state have little experience of working together and little capacity to do so, and even less experience of working flexibly with local government. Ensuring that people are involved in making the agreement has the personal and practical benefit of limiting contracts to those which people value. What most people want, especially when feeling vulnerably dependent on the care of strangers, is a secure feeling that the public service is going to be on their side. They want to feel, in a sense, the confidence in the NHS that comes from seeing it in action on 'Casualty', rather than the 'Price is Right' or 'LA Law'. Without public confidence, service contract or not, the struggle necessary to establish a real right to service may not seem worth the trouble.

The current debate about the public service, following as it does on a decade of devastation, may be creating a context where democracy experiences a renewal. Contracts play a part in that process, not only by effecting practical changes in service but also by encouraging and reinforcing a political culture which is attentive to and respectful of individuality. It may gain some popularity in the process.

Decentralised structures make it easier to involve people and open up organisations and professions to different ways of meeting people's needs, listening to their preferences, and demonstrating the value of their services. Equal opportunities policies, and the social groups who argue for them, also make it more likely that public services will not systematically oppress or ignore particular social groups. Such policies may not be preconditions for empowering residents and users in every locality, but they create opportunities and access that otherwise would not exist. What must be avoided are the ideas of one group in society constructing a set of rights for the rest.

National movements may feel impatient with the local and rather messy approach to empowering citizens which is described here. The temptation to seek greater social equity through the use of centralised instruments of national government, such as the law, may be very strong. I have argued that such shortcuts are more apparent than real. Sooner or later, ideas and laws have to come out and explain their relevance to the public.

No renewal of public services, no matter how brilliant the ideas, will be achieved by providing everyone with the same service rights or identical set of entitlements no matter how generous. People need to be practically involved in order to make public services work, and be seen to be working. Service contracts negotiated at community level between local authorities and local residents offer one way of bringing this about.

8 RIGHTS OF CHILDREN AND YOUNG PEOPLE

Priscilla Alderson

Rights are claimed effectively by people whose voices are heard, but who listens to children? Traditions at every level of society ensure that they are not heard: from arrangements in health, education and social services, to common beliefs about children's inabilities and incompetence.

This chapter begins by reviewing recent changes in the law on children's rights. It considers the key role of decision-making and consent in defining and asserting children's rights. It then describes ways in which children are not seen and not heard, and examines definitions of children in relation to their competence to make and consent to decisions. A new approach to defining children is proposed. This chapter explores the relationship between rights and needs as this particularly affects children, and considers how rights can conflict. Finally, it examines ways in which a framework of rights for a modern welfare system can be extended to children, to liberate them or protect them. By raising questions about children's rights, needs and abilities, the chapter aims to promote public discussion as a first stage in extending the framework of welfare rights to take proper account of children.

Children's rights in law

Children's rights in English law have been dramatically revised recently, partly because of the case of Mrs Victoria Gillick, who took her health authority to court in the mid-1980s.[1] She wanted the court to rule that children under 16-years old in general, and her five daughters in particular, could not obtain medical treatment without their parents' knowledge and consent. She was mainly concerned to stop children's access to treatment and advice about contraception.

The legal right which Mrs Gillick hoped to block arose in the 1969 Family Law Reform Act which states that children aged 16 and over can automatically give effective consent to medical treatment; their parents' consent is therefore not necessary. The Act was silent on the under-16s' right to consent. Mrs Gillick wanted the court to make a clear ruling that minors under 16 years cannot give consent to medical treatment.

The case went through several hearings and some judges agreed with Mrs Gillick. However, the Law Lords finally ruled that English law is concerned with each child's understanding, rather than with age. Children of any age may consent, which includes the option to refuse treatment, when they are able 'fully to understand what is proposed'.

The 1989 Children Act confirms this principle, stating that children may refuse to submit to medical or psychiatric examination or other assessment 'if they have sufficient understanding to make informed decisions'. The Act repeatedly states that in decision-making, 'the child's wishes and feelings' should be ascertained, but it makes this part of a list of procedures which stress parents' responsibilities. The 1975 Children Act and the 1980 Child Care Act (Section 18) state more firmly that children in care must be consulted. The 1989 Act extends the child's right to be consulted to certain institutional child protection and court procedures, but does not cover many other services affecting children.

The Gillick ruling opens the way for children to have the right to be consulted seriously about all decisions which personally affect them: decisions about medical treatment, surgery and health care, residence and contact with their parents, their education, religion, and other decisions affecting their welfare. However, the Children Act only states that children's views should be taken into account, not that they should be observed. Children's interests, and not their rights, are paramount, and interests are usually decided by adults.

The Gillick case shows how Victorian beliefs about children contrast with those of the present. A century ago, children were seen mainly as their father's property. People under 21 years were legally 'infants', literally meaning without a voice; they had to depend on adults to decide and speak on their behalf. However, the Gillick ruling emphasised that, today, parents only have rights over their children insofar as these enable parents to fulfil their responsibility to care for the child. These 'dwindling rights', as Lord Denning described them in 1970, yield to the child's growing competence.[2] Another important influence has been the 1989 United Nations Convention on the Rights of the Child. The Conservative Government and the Labour Party (in 1992) are committed to ratifying this internationally agreed set of principles to guide law, policy and practice for children. The Convention covers rights to resources and protection, and confirms that civil rights must apply to children. For example, they should have freedom of expression, freedom of thought, conscience and religion, and freedom of association.[3]

> The child who is capable of forming his or her own views [shall be assured] the right to express those views freely in all matters affecting the child, the views of the child shall be given due weight in

accordance with the age and maturity of the child.[4]
This means that children must be heard in any judicial or administrative proceedings, either directly or through a representative.

English law in the Gillick case recognises the child's right to self-determination more fully than does the UN Convention. The Convention does not replace or invalidate domestic laws which are 'more conducive to the rights of the child'.[5] Children's rights in Britain will have a strong legal basis when the Convention is ratified and combined with present legal statements on their rights.

Rights and consent

The right to consent has an impact on all other rights. Consent is about selecting options, negotiating them, and accepting or rejecting them. Beyond making a decision, consent is about making an informed choice and becoming emotionally committed to it. Consent can only happen when there is no force or coercion. It is about deciding one's own best interests and preferences; it determines whether children can decide which rights they prefer to have, or whether adults choose for them. This can happen on a general or an individual level.

Rights are selected on a general level when, for instance, adults enshrine them in charters and laws, or omit certain rights. Children may emphasise rights which are different from those which adults would choose for them. This was illustrated by an assembly of 500 children held by the United Nations concurrently with the adult assembly in Geneva in 1989. The youngest group, those aged six to eight years, voted for the right to choose their own leisure activities and to help weaker people. The nine to 12-year-olds voted for the right to have a good environment, and to help the less well-off. Those aged 13 years and over voted to be listened to, to give opinions and to take their place in society.[6]

Apart from differences on a general level between children's and adults' choice of rights, individual children experience conflicts of rights. For instance, there is often a conflict between adequate protection and reasonable freedom. This is shown in arguments about whether children should have the right to do paid work, or to be protected from the potential exploitation of child labour. Beliefs about the best way to care for children and to balance their conflicting rights vary radically over time, and between individuals; seeking children's consent is a way of involving them in deciding the best balance. The child's choice may differ from that of the adults.

Children's ability to consent depends partly upon whether they can speak for themselves, or at least as partners *with* their advocates, or whether adults speak entirely *for* them. Asserting a right in a sense denotes a claim by, or at least with, the right-holders. Can rights which are entirely decided and imposed by adults on children correctly be defined as rights? For example, adults often say that a child has a right to a good upbringing. Yet this right has been interpreted in cruel as well as positive ways by adults through the centuries.[7] It might be better expressed as a set of duties, imposed by adults on themselves and on children.

Children too young to speak and give formal consent may seem to be denied any rights, in the strict sense of a right as a right-holder's assertion. Yet in its widest sense, consent could be taken to include unspoken responses. The sight and sound of a starving baby can be interpreted as a plea for certain types of treatment, and a rejection of other types – a plea which can be as urgent and eloquent as intellectual argument.

Rethinking childhood in terms of rights opens the way for children to be consulted more fully in defining their interests. Taking consent seriously is one means of attempting this. When adults are certain that they know best and that children are incapable of being reasoned with, forcing a child to comply is often considered acceptable. Yet this legitimates violence and child abuse. The wider recognition of children's rights is a crucial means of combatting these problems.

The consent process is a means of enabling children to be heard, as well as to speak; these can be quite separate activities. There is talk of giving a voice to children. Yet children have voices and plenty of opinions. They need adults to listen. People who accept children's right to consent accept that at least sometimes they can be competent, that is, informed, wise and worth listening to.

Acknowledging children

The US Constitution asserts the right of everyone to 'life, liberty and security of person'. Similarly, the Universal Declaration of Human Rights in 1948 asserted the right of all human beings 'to live out their lives in freedom from fear and want'. Article 25 stated that 'everyone has the right to a standard of living adequate for the health and well-being of himself and his family, including food, clothing, housing and medical care and necessary social services.'

Immediately the question arises, who is 'everyone'? At what age do we begin to count as 'someone'? Has a very premature baby weighing only as much as half a bag of sugar a right to very costly medical care? The care might save her life, but she is likely to survive only with severe disabilities. It has been argued that newborn babies do not have any right to life,[8] and that, for some very ill children and adults, their right to life conflicts with their right to die when life becomes intolerable.[9]

At the other end of childhood, the new born baby's responsible adults may include a 13-year-old mother with parental rights. Yet the choices open to her may be illusory. Like other pregnant adolescents, she may be constrained to choose to end her pregnancy because she does not have resources which are available to many adult women.

Many rights such as the right to survive depend, of course, on resources. If parents of any age have few resources, their offspring are at risk of counting less as someone with a right to survive. Poorer children, and they include a disproportionate number of those from ethnic minorities, are far more likely to be born too small and early, and to have gross disabilities, fatal illness and accidents.

Teenage parenthood is often criticised on the ground that adolescents' immaturity makes them harmful and unhappy parents; their own development can only be damaged by such responsibility; they have no right to the basic resources which caring parents need. This chapter is not advocating teenage parenthood. As the IPPR report, *The Family Way* argues, girls need better educational and career opportunities so that motherhood is no longer seen by many, however unconsciously, as the only means to escape tedious, humiliating dependence.[10]

However, objections to teenage parenthood beg questions about children's maturity and abilities, their dependence and relationships, their developmental and resource needs, and rights. If we are to attend to children and listen to their views seriously, then each of these issues has to be examined. For instance, does bearing quite heavy responsibility for themselves and for others harm children? Children can assume heavy responsibilities at work, in the home, and in caring for other children and many children in Britain play a large part in caring for sick or disabled relatives.

Children's rights entail both freedom and responsibility, as they take over from their parents and, in a sense, become their own parent or caretaker. Many will argue that teenagers cannot and should not do this, at least under 16-years of age. Yet, as we have seen, the law takes another view: children can be responsible for personal decisions when adults judge that they are competent to do so. Before considering at what age they are likely to become competent, we need to ask who children are.

Defining 'children'

The usual format in rights documents is to group all young people within an age limit, such as:

A child means every human being below the age of 18-years unless, under the law applicable to the child, majority is attained earlier.[11]

In all parts of the world, the most oppressed, needy and forgotten social groups include children. Defining them by age usefully draws attention to them as a distinct, vulnerable group. It also emphasises that many children have particular needs which differ from adult needs.

Yet the definition presents problems. It complicates questions about abortion and embryo research issues when the foetus is included with 'everyone under 18'. It denies the way in which children are reaching physical maturity much earlier than in past centuries. It ignores the legal trend away from enforcing a single age of majority. For example, English law now allows various freedoms to children, at five, seven, 12 years, and so on.[12] Most importantly, the age definition works against the kind of progress seen in the law, moving away from specifying any particular age, towards *acknowledging each individual child's developing competence.*

Classifying all under-18s as children wrongly implies that mature adolescents have more in common with babies than with adults. This can silence all children. Movements for other formerly unheard groups, such as women and black people, campaigned against the injustices that result when others presume to speak for them and to decide their needs. We now need to consider how far children are able to speak for themselves in an adult way.

A further disadvantage of putting everyone under 18 years into a single group is that the group is mainly negatively defined as non-adult. In the last few decades, women have drawn attention to the way language which seems neutral and inclusive is actually covertly dismissive of women, or hostile towards them. In the same way, much literature, which is enlightened towards adults, on careful reading is seen to be covertly unfair to children. Rights charters which assert respect and dignity, the right to work and to vote for everyone, but have no intention of including children in 'everyone' offer examples of such discrimination. Children are not only denied rights, but are implicitly classed as non-persons.

Concern for children's rights tends to be delegated to women. Yet as the philosopher Judith Hughes points out, this is not necessarily helpful to children. She notes a certain cynicism among women:

> who rightly suspect that proposed liberal reforms, such as allowing
> children to decide whether or not to go to school . . . will leave
> [women] as practitioners of those reforms.[13]

Judith Hughes accepts that many arguments denigrating children were used until recently against women. Women are therefore wary of using them against children. Yet women and black people:

> did not spend a couple of centuries arguing that we were not children
> but adults, simply to be told that, in that case, children are too.

Some distinction between adults and dependent young children is obviously needed. But distinctions which are too sweeping and rigid can be destructive. They appeal to simplistic prejudice, such as the tendency to attribute all wisdom, maturity, knowledge and prudence to the adult, and therefore all folly, ignorance and self-destructiveness to the child. Already disadvantaged by inexperience, children frequently endure the further disability of being encrusted with, even obscured by, unjust prejudices about their weakness and inabilities.

Children's ability to understand

In a study by this author on children's consent to surgery,[14] patients aged eight to 15 years and the adults caring for them were interviewed. They were asked at what age they thought children were able to understand the details about their proposed treatment, and around which age they could be trusted to make wise decisions about it. The replies from every group, patients, parents and professionals, ranged from early childhood to early adulthood, and revealed as much about the respondent as about ages of competence.

Some parents and children thought that certain young children could have a mature understanding of their illness and treatment. Professionals working very closely with children, such as a psychologist and a play specialist, spontaneously described unusual three, four and five-year-olds who, they thought, showed remarkable understanding and maturity. Other professionals could think of no examples, and said that understanding was impossible until 16, 18 years, or even older. A teacher in an adolescent ward commented: 'Of course they have *no* conception of what is happening to them'. A family doctor said: 'It's unfair when parents send any child under 16 years to the doctor on his own. It puts far too much responsibility on the doctor'.

One psychologist remarked: 'My developmental training tells me that it would be quite wrong to burden any child with the responsibility of making a choice about medical treatment. Adults must decide for them.' This 'developmental training' was a reference to theories that children's mental and moral capacities develop in stages, like the stages of physical development. Psychologists such as Jean Piaget taught that children are rarely able to grasp certain concepts before the age of seven or 11 years. He demonstrated that children could not show where one place on three mountains was invisible from other places. He then inferred that children under seven years were unable to appreciate another person's viewpoint.[15] Lawrence Kohlberg believed that there are six stages of moral development, and few people can reach the highest stage.[16]

If these masters were right, there would be little point in trying to involve young children in thinking about rights or consent, because they would be unable to grasp the basic cognitive and moral concepts. However, later studies challenge the earlier ideas. Psychologists such as Margaret Donaldson have shown that three-year-olds can solve the puzzles which older children failed to solve with

Piaget; and they can solve more complex puzzles as well, if these are presented in ways that arouse their interest – such as when the abstract mountain points are changed into a game of naughty boys hiding from a policeman.[17] Carol Gilligan found much evidence to confirm Kohlberg's view that many people, mainly women, stop at his third moral stage of personal compassion and concern for individual experience.[18] But she questioned his conclusions that their morality is inferior, and that abstract universal principles and respect for lonely autonomy are the highest form of morality. Gilligan argued that the personal morality of many pre-puberty children and many adults is as valuable and mature as more impersonal forms of morality, and they are not just stuck in a childish phase as Kohlberg believed. Young children's complex awareness of material and moral concepts, and the potential value of consulting them are becoming more widely recognised. Yet as long as some child care professionals continue to preach discredited theories, and generalise about all children's supposed inabilities, the general public is unlikely to adopt more liberal views.

Children's silence

The children's advocate, John Holt, thinks that the child is seen as 'super-pet, slave or expensive nuisance':[19] three silent roles. (Although a nuisance may be noisy, by definition it is not worth hearing.) He points out that adults protest against 'being treated like a child', but no one protests about how unpleasant this can be for children. Unlike adults, children are regularly punished for talking, and behaving in ways which adults take for granted as a right. Respect for children's pure innocence can be a kindness or a dangerous cage. Jenny Kitzinger, a sociologist, shows how mass-media reports of child sexual abuse disempower children by portraying them either as helpless dolls or as assertive young girls who are seen no longer as innocent, but as guilty accomplices in the abuse. Children are thus trapped into silence or vain protest. Their supposed helplessness or guilt prevent them from being respected or heard by adults.[20]

When their protests are not attended to, many children feel forced to act, by flight or fight. One example is eight-year-old Lester, who died after running away from home for the fourth time, because of daily beatings.[21] After his earlier attempts to escape, the police found lesions on him which would have amounted to grievous bodily harm to an adult. However, the law entitles parents to hit their children, and a doctor described the injuries as 'trivial', so the police took him back home. Lester's clear statements that he would rather die than stay at home went unheard.

An estimated 150,000 16- to 19-year-olds experience homelessness each year. Those who have formerly been in care are forty times more likely than other young people to be homeless for a time.[22] Rarely able to find paid work, these homeless children, in effect, become out-laws, breaking the vagrancy, begging and soliciting laws in order to survive. A further 150,000 younger children were in families statutorily accepted as homeless in 1989.[23] Increasingly, children make up a large part of the unseen, unheard population living in poverty.

Black children are greatly over-represented among the homeless, and those in care. 'There is a worrying over-representation of black children in the controlling aspects of child protection work and under-representation in the welfare aspects.'[24] This comment by Bandana Ahmed suggests that children's initial pleas for help, when the caring agencies could help them, go unheard. They are not noticed until they resort to behaviour which is regarded as delinquent and requiring control and punishment. Like abused children, they are caught between silence or vain protest. There is double jeopardy when racism and sexism are compounded for children by ageism.

Children are silenced in many contexts. Efforts to listen to them in the courts[25] and social services[26] illustrate the many barriers which have to be painstakingly dismantled before children can be heard. The barriers include traditions which intimidate and exclude children, the lack of skilled adults to talk with them, widespread attitudes among adults that youngsters cannot and should not be consulted because they are too stupid, ignorant or confused, and many young people's angry despair that they will not be believed.

In the research about children's consent to surgery it was found that some children preferred their parents to decide for them. Others carefully weighed the harms of surgery against the benefits they hoped to obtain. Some children remained determined throughout months of painful treatment which they had chosen to undertake. Some chose, despite their parents' advice, to continue with a series of operations. 'They'll go through tremendous levels of pain to achieve what they want to,' said one father.[27]

Some decisions seem reckless, but have been carefully evaluated. One view is not necessarily wrong and the other right. As one doctor remarked, decision in medicine often 'remains a hope, *a best guess*, and an act of faith' (his emphasis).[28] Decisions in many other areas of the child's life are also often a best guess. They are informed decisions if the child's, as well as the adults', views are considered. However, society has a long way to go before children in general are heard with respect.

Childhood as a status, not a state

Defining someone as a 'child' introduces conflicting assumptions. Children's immaturity is considered to entitle them to extra resources (free health checks, schools, playgrounds). Yet their immaturity denies them other entitlements (the right to vote, to earn an income, and so on). So adults' rights can be seen, for children, as both too few and too many.

Increasingly, the law recognises that many children have adult capacities. Appropriate protection for one child is inappropriate coercion for another, or even for the same child in a different context. It would therefore be clearer, in relation to public policies, to see childhood as a *status* rather than a *state*. A 'state' is taken to mean something complete, inescapable and unchangeable, such as a state of physical immaturity. A child is a child until reaching the birthday when adulthood begins. Nothing but time can alter the state. A status is more social and variable, acknowledged to be something conferred from outside; it is how you are perceived or labelled rather than how you are. It is partial and changeable.

For example, a boy of 13 years has the status of a child with regard to drinking in pubs, but of an adult in a pet shop (12-year-olds are legally entitled to buy a pet).[29] The status of a foetus varies as to whether it is in an antenatal clinic or an abortion clinic. A baby, in constant need of nurture and protection, has the status of a child in almost every respect. A capable girl of eight-years is classed as a child in relation to driving on public roads but as an adult if she can consent competently to medical treatment.

Between the child who is protected and nurtured, and the adult who chooses and acts independently by right, there is a middle position of emerging independence. This could be called the status of being a young person. The eight-year-old acts as a young person in being able to consent, as long as she can demonstrate her competence, but she does not have the adult's unquestioned right to consent. When pre-schoolers' choices, such as about clothes, friends or activities, are respected by their parents, they have the status of young people in these matters, free within boundaries set by adults. In Britain, full adulthood is not acknowledged until 25 years, since young people have disadvantages, such as lower social security payments, and advantages, such as lower rail fares.

In this chapter, the word 'children' is used in the general sense for people of pre-school and school age. It is also used in a particular sense to refer to people who need protection, resources, and advocates to speak for them and to decide their best interests. 'Young people' usually means those who do not have full, automatic adult rights. They share certain substantive rights with children or adults, and are learning to decide, speak and act for themselves. They need advocates to work with them, rather than for them. 'Adults' means people of any age who have adult rights and responsibilities in relation to the policy being discussed. They need advocates or expert advisers only as much as other similar adults would. Rights can be examined for how they affect youngsters as children, young people or as adults. Denying adult status to children, because of tradition or prejudice, needs to be justified and sometimes changed.

Defining and debating rights

Adults' claims

Before the 1960s, experts frankly disregarded children's opinions and few claimed to be advocating rights, although many claimed to know the right or correct practice. Since the 1960s the concept of 'rights' has become a popular form for rephrasing moral claims, once expressed in terms of the child's own good.

Some rights are claims that powerful groups should grant greater liberty or resources to less powerful groups, and children are the least powerful social group. They need adults to be involved in defining and asserting rights on their behalf. Yet when this is done entirely by adults, it implies that adults' ideals are shared by children – and this prevents children's own distinct views from being recognised.

Speaking about children's rights in terms of adults' duties at least recognises that adults have powerful discretion over how they choose to fulfil, or fail in, their obligation towards the child. A 'duty' sounds less binding and enforceable than a 'right'. The language of duties is possibly more truthful about the reality of adults' power and children's dependence; relations between adult and child are often better understood in terms of the adult's rights over the child. Yet the language of children's rights can embody hopes for the future, because it opens the way to involving children in asserting their own rights.

There is danger in talking about rights in the wrong context. If the right-holders are not adequately consulted, rights language can be more oppressive than other terminology. This is because talking about rights suggests freedom and choice, but when these are missing, 'rights' can be a euphemism for quite repressive claims about what adults think children ought to have but may not want. To describe an adult's opinion as a child's right can gloss over and disguise coercion, and this kind of power is greatest when it is least visible.[30] Take, for example, the child-care experts who stress small children's 'right to stimulation'. As advice, it may be beneficial, but it can also help to generate a costly and oppressive baby-stimulation industry.

The words 'rights' and 'needs' are sometimes used as though they were interchangeable; both can lend a spurious objectivity to claims based on the personal beliefs of 'experts'. The psychologist Martin Woodhead suggests that 'need' is shorthand for: *as an expert I think this is what you need and there should be a law about it.*[31] He cites one such claim, the child's 'need' for continuous one-to-one mothering care in the early years; critics of the claim argue that young children can enjoy security with a range of carers, and even escape the disadvantages and dangers of being isolated with bored, lonely parents.

However, in justly challenging over-blown claims about needs, there is a risk of denying the existence of need altogether. Woodhead, for example, suggests that 'our understanding and respect for childhood might be better served if "children's needs" were outlawed from future professional discourse, policy recommendations and popular psychology'. But the problem then is to suggest that children do not have serious needs, and that everything can be classed simply as a personal claim, based on arbitrary values which completely differ in time and place. And if everything is changeable and thus dispensable, does anything seriously matter? And if nothing matters, what is the point of respecting children's rights to ephemeral, unnecessary unrealities?

Rights, reason and need

Valid human rights have, like the UN Convention on the Rights of the Child,[32] to start from need, and from realities such as the illness and death, injury and abandonment of millions of children annually. The term 'rights' began to be used in the modern sense only a few centuries ago, and only in relation to property-owning men.[33] Post-feudal philosophers argued that men's political and property rights ought to be respected because they were capable of 'pure reason'.[34] As rational beings, they should be able to determine their own lives. The first rights to be asserted therefore concerned liberties and non-interference with men's autonomy. Rights were justified in terms of appropriate respect for the highest human good – reason.

Women and children were seen as emotional, and therefore irrational and not entitled to rights.[35] They also tended to be seen as man's property, and necessarily dependent and under his rational control. There is still a very strong link between rights and reason, between having the right to choose and having the ability to choose rightly. So, for example, when people are judged to choose wrongly they are diagnosed or convicted as being irrational, as mad or bad, and have to forfeit certain rights. The view of some philosophers that pre-verbal children have no right to life is based on the argument that they have no language and therefore no reason, and that only rational beings can have rights.[36]

In response to the emphasis on rationality, there are two bases for justifying rights for women, black people, children, prisoners, the mentally ill and everyone else who was originally disenfranchised by the 'pure reason' argument. One is to argue that they too are rational and are therefore entitled to equal rights on the basis of their reason. This is frequently true. Yet as Judith Hughes remarked: 'If rational is what nineteenth-century gentlemen are, then children no less than women will come to grief in the rationality stakes.'[37] The other response is to justify rights on the basis of need. People's rights should be respected in order to prevent serious physical or mental harm to them, and to ensure that their needs are met.

The 'pure reason' basis for rights respects people who are rational and not emotional. As one philosopher, Victor Seidler, wrote critically, this ideal splits apart the worlds of reason and of feeling. Only in the rational world are our freedom and autonomy guaranteed to us, because in the feeling world we are driven and constrained by our needs, desires and human inadequacy. We can only become rational when we rise above feeling and need.[38]

The unduly rational approach unwittingly provides three vital reasons for justifying children's (and everyone's) rights on the basis of their need rather than their reason. First it is unrealistic. No-one is purely rational and pretending to be so can be a convenient way of disguising one's own self-interest. Second, there are strong arguments (as Raymond Plant demonstrates in Chapter 1) for extending rights to liberty and non-interference to include rights to resources and protection – and these concern our physical need as much as our reason. Third, because needs arise in the feeling world and not simply in the rational world, they therefore cannot be understood through reason alone.

Needs are profoundly understood beyond reason, through pain and pleasure. Through the experience, say, of being hated because of their colour, people gain unique insight into their own needs and rights. Adults working with seriously ill children speak of them as becoming 'very wise through their suffering'.[39] There is concern that abused children are cognitively and emotionally retarded, and are therefore more than usually dependent on adults to make decisions for them. Yet although they may be slower in some respects, they have above-average knowledge about the harms they feel in submitting to unwanted adult activities. The refusal of very young, abused children to submit, for example, to medical examinations, should therefore be taken at least as seriously as the refusal of adults who do not have this personal knowledge.

The rationality basis regards only highly qualified (usually healthy, white) professionals as able to decide about the rights of sick or black children. The needs basis acknowledges that children's experience and wisdom beyond rationality earn them a rightful and essential part in making decisions that affect them. Feelings and experience qualify rather than disqualify people when understanding and asserting their rights. A society that respects people's bodies and feelings, instead of implicitly denigrating them in over-reverence for rationality, is likely to be a kinder and more equal society. Rights based on reason alone are elitist and at odds with the egalitarian intentions of human rights movements.

Absolute and relative rights

Rights based in absolute physical and mental need are intended to help to prevent death and severe injury. This is the grounding for the universal human *rights to survival*, such as the right to clean water. Minimal wellbeing is also an absolute need, covered by the *rights to protection* from abuse and neglect. The UN Convention on the Rights of the Child includes a third group of rights, headed the *right to develop*, through play, education and health care. These rights include the opportunity to share in 'the social, economic, religious and political life of the culture – free from discrimination'.[40] The last set of rights seems to move beyond absolute into relative need in two ways: they are not essential to bare survival, and they vary in their expression between cultures. Yet survival, protection and development rights all range through the spectrum of levels of need, from minimal survival to flourishing, and they overlap in many complex ways. Feeding a baby inevitably involves some kind of human contact, however minimal, which draws the child into the social, economic, religious and political culture. The baby begins to have expectations, whether in a Beverley Hills mansion, a hut in Soweto, or a Romanian orphanage. Rights to survival cannot be divorced from rights to develop a shared social life.

Relative rights which vary between cultures, such as the right to watch television, may seem trivial. They are cited as derisory examples to dismiss the whole concept of children's rights, either as nonsense, or as dangerously subversive. Such dismissal should be questioned. First, it reflects adults' rather than children's values, assuming that only adult values count. Second, it ignores the way in which relative rights may be founded in more basic rights.

Children stress normality – looking like their friends and being able to do the same things. In the research project on children's consent to surgery, they are asked how they hope their operation will help them. 'It'll make me look more normal', and 'I'll be able to do normal things again, like going out with my friends' are typical replies. They also talk about the pain and loneliness of being different, even in seemingly small ways, like not being able to play football, or not being allowed to watch a television serial which their friends see – differences which are crucial to the child concerned.

Possessions and opportunities, which would be luxuries in one culture, are embedded in another culture so deeply that children see them as essential to their welfare. One example is the right to dress similarly enough to one's friends as not to be rejected by them. Expressing the desire to be normal in terms of a 'right' can be criticised as facile support for a greedy consumer ethic. Yet perceived from the child's viewpoint, 'normal' clothing powerfully affects mental health and the right to share 'in the social. . .life of the culture without discrimination'.[41]

The 1989 Children Act requires that 'due consideration be given to the child's religious preferences, racial origins, and cultural and linguistic back-ground' (although only in relation to local authority decisions for children they are looking after). Yet if, as a general principle, children are to work in partnership with the adults and agencies caring for them then, as the Act repeatedly states, their 'wishes and feelings' must be attended to. In order to be able to select and assert their rights, children need to have a sense of personal identity and self-esteem, based on links with their family and friends, their past, present and future, their culture and religion. Asserting rights can be a struggle for many adults, and is still harder for inexperienced children. Children in care, for example, gain strength through joining organisations that identify their particular needs, such as the 'National Association for Young People in Care', and 'Black and in Care'.

Grand principles, such as rights to freedom, acquire real meaning when they are practised in numerous, although often tiny, ways. The more detail in which rights are laid down, the more rigidly and narrowly people will be expected to conform, a paradox which ends by depriving them of basic freedoms of choice. Yet broad claims, such as the right to dignity, are interpreted in such disparate ways that unless partly qualified they are meaningless. Rights are open to varying interpretations – for example, the right to protection from abuse and physical punishment which is 'cruel, inhuman or degrading':[42] the effects of punishment would be assessed differently by the child receiving it and the adults inflicting it. Therefore, instead of society determining the details, and declaring which rights are major or minor, absolute or relative, the children concerned could share in deciding, within a clear framework of rights.

Protection versus independence

Rights to survival and protection can conflict with rights to develop independently, for example, by making choices about diet or education. Some experts take a gloomy view of allowing children to exercise autonomy on the ground that it exposes them to abuse by other people, and to self-abuse through immature folly. The lawyer John Eekelaar comments: when a child has reached competence, there is no room for a parent to impose a contrary view, *even if this is more in accord with the child's best interests*' (his emphasis).[43] He wonders whether 'inhibition up to a defined age' such as 16 years would not be better, instead of allowing younger children to make decisions, 'in case the failure to exercise restraint unduly prejudices a person's basic or developmental interests?' However, he stresses that 'capacity' includes maturity in making wise choices, and he concludes that 'children will now have, in wider measure than ever before, that most dangerous but precious of rights: the right to make their own mistakes'. Others take a more robust view, saying that the only way to learn to exercise autonomy is by practice, and by making some mistakes. Few decisions are so major and irrevocable that the child will be seriously harmed by mistakes, and age is no safeguard since adults, too, make plenty of errors.

Laws on child labour illustrate the conflict between protection and liberty. Children need legal protection from being exploited by employers. Yet over-protection that prevents them from earning any income traps them into complete dependence on possibly abusive caretakers, or into working illegally, or begging. The law therefore needs to balance the right to protection with the right to independence, since each offers security and abuse. Laws designed to protect youngsters by forbidding child labour result in children working illegally, with no state help in negotiating fair pay and safe conditions, no union, inspectorate, insurance, or other support that adult workers have. A survey in 1991 found that a quarter of children in paid work are aged 12 years or less, though paid work is illegal for under 13-year-olds, and they are the most badly exploited.[44]

The right to work is related to children's health and welfare in several ways. Health and welfare correlate with poverty, which can give some children good cause to work and to earn a better standard of living. Yet poverty is also a consequence of child labour, when children are too tired to learn at school, and leave school as soon as possible, in order to earn. They are then unlikely to qualify for jobs with higher pay.

Work also has a negative effect in that work-related illness and injury are major causes of poverty for adults and their children. Children's rights are affected by their parents' poverty. Working conditions are one of many instances demonstrating how children's rights are more likely to be respected when society is also more respectful towards adults. If everyone enjoyed reasonable conditions at work, rights to protection from abuse at work and rights to freedom to work need not conflict.[45]

Social and economic rights should be seen in relation to civil and political ones since the former are often a precondition for the exercise of the latter. Children's civil rights are in an embryonic stage, similar to that of women's rights a century ago. It is beyond the scope of this chapter to consider the complex debates surrounding children's civil rights. However, by concentrating on social rights it is not my intention to imply that children are only capable of receiving benefits and protection, or that their rights to liberty are less important.

Health and welfare rights

Many health and welfare rights for adults, discussed in the rest of this book, also apply to young people and children, so this section will consider rights and services mainly as they particularly affect youngsters. The central themes are:

* the effects of integrated or fragmented services;
* the tension between rights to privacy and to protection;
* the apparent conflict between rights to respect and also to care, when care is intrusive.

Integrating services

Respected policy documents, such as the Court Report,[46] repeatedly show how children suffer when seen from separate professional viewpoints (health, welfare, education, housing, and so on) instead of being looked at as a whole child. Harmful effects of discrimination in one area are missed unless the whole welfare state is reviewed. Of course, adults also suffer when services are fragmented. Yet children are often even less able to point out gaps and contradictions between services, or to be heard by the many professionals concerned. The Warnock Report on integrating children with disabilities into ordinary schools[47] stresses the need for a key worker to co-ordinate services, as do other reports. Nurses similarly advise that each patient in hospital should have a primary nurse, who helps to represent the patient's views, and tries to ensure that all the hospital professionals are accountable to the patient.

Some children stay in hospital for weeks, because their consultants consider that the schooling, physiotherapy, or psychotherapy in hospital is better than in the community services. The decision may be presented to the family as a clinical one, rather than the social decision it is. Respect for children's private life would involve different medical training, enabling doctors to recognise children's social needs more fully (as many of them already do) and to share such decisions with families. It would involve returning to more integrated child health services, in which community services adequately complement hospital ones.

One example of the problems resulting from fragmented services is the way children are particularly in danger of traffic accidents. Wearing a brightly coloured coat is an effective safeguard, and popular with youngsters. Yet frequently it is indirectly illegal. By law, children must attend school regularly, but head teachers can ban them from school if they do not wear the uniform, which often includes a plain, dark coat. Parents who do not make their children wear the uniform can be taken to court and may be found guilty of permitting truancy.

A children's rights policy should examine the sense and safety of school uniform rules, including those which lead to Muslim girls being banned from school for wearing scarves or trousers for religious reasons. More important is the relationship between school teachers and the people they teach. How would the principle to treat youngsters whenever possible as sensible young people, rather than as immature children, transform schools? Why are so many automatic rights for adults denied to young people at school? And how does the denial affect efforts to educate youngsters as active, questioning members of a humane democracy?

Neighbourhood forums or councils made up of children, parents and professionals could tap the valuable knowledge of people using the services. They could advise on creating child-friendly environments, and help to reduce vandalism and accidents. But to do so they would have to try to overcome the relative power of adults (particularly professionals) and the weakness of the clients (particularly children). It would be necessary to experiment and search for the right mechanisms, and to accept that these are likely to be imperfect.

Privacy versus protection

> Everyone has the right to a standard of living adequate for the health
> and well-being of himself and his family, including food, clothing,
> housing and medical care and necessary social services.[48]

Statements about rights written for adults present problems for children. Children's rights to 'necessary services' can conflict with parents' rights to privacy. When should the state intervene if children are deprived through their parents' poverty or deliberate neglect? How seriously does child abuse have to be suspected before social workers intrude into the family home? People from all parts of the political spectrum criticise or advocate state intervention in the family when abuse is suspected, for a range of complex reasons.[49]

The present practice of tending to remove the abused child, instead of the abuser, respects the adults' liberties over the child's. If this practice were to change and the reverse become routine, the police would need to support court orders more stringently, protecting homes against the return of abusers. Yet this kind of policing will alter relations between the police and the public. Whether to make such changes, and how best to introduce them, requires careful analysis. Respecting the family home entails restricting certain individual freedoms.

Children's rights to health can also conflict with parents' rights to privacy. 'Health' can range in meaning from freedom from disease, to (as a woman dying in exile of TB wrote) 'the power to live a full, adult living breathing life in close contact with what I love . . . all that I am capable of becoming'.[50] The health of dependent children is affected by their parents' nurturing, and by how far the state intervenes if parents are unable or unwilling to care for their children adequately.

Lawyers such as John Eekelaar argue that parents have only a negative legal duty of care to avoid depriving their children; there is not a positive duty on them to pursue 'maximum promotion of health'.[51] This is because parent-child relationships are too private, complex and personal to be regulated by detailed legislation. However, according to sociologist Berry Mayall, one form of state intervention – health visiting – is not only about safeguarding against parental care falling below 'normal' standards, but also about finding ways of raising it to 'higher' standards as defined by health visitors.[52] This is a contentious matter. Parents easily feel threatened by professional observers, and this can adversely affect fragile, volatile family relationships. Health and social services have to achieve a delicate balance between working for the child but, as far as possible, with the parents, supporting the family without undermining it, until the point when criticism is seen as essential protection from serious danger to the child.

Professionals have to decide when to treat parents as their main, although proxy clients, and when to treat the child as their client, if necessary against the parents' wishes. Unlike services for adult clients, those for children have to take into account two related but sometimes conflicting perspectives: the *child-as-an-individual* and the *child-in-the-family*. Different classes and ethnic groups vary in their beliefs about how conflicts between individual versus family and community interests should be balanced.

Rights to respect and to care

As we have seen, human rights were first designated as civil and political rights, stressing respect for the autonomy of the independent man and non-interference with his property and daily life. Children's social and economic rights concern protection and care, and often depend on the opposite response – active interference on behalf of vulnerable people. In its older, narrow meaning, respect as non-interference can seem irrelevant to dependent children. Consequently there is a danger that children's autonomy may be denied, and their dignity, privacy and any ability to decide their own best interests ignored until they reach adult independence.

Very sick or young people are most in need of protection, which can sometimes be intrusive: in their case particularly, respect requires a richer meaning in which dignity and need are both carefully attended to. Life-sustaining intrusion is balanced with respect for privacy while freedom of choice is balanced with being able to opt out of making decisions, or with having a greater or lesser share in making them. Instead of being a standard, impersonal formula for the mythical autonomous man, respect becomes a sensitive and, if mutually wished for, an intimate relationship between unique individuals.

The balance is particularly difficult where children are concerned, because they are usually powerless in relation to adults, and their parents are often joint, rival, or proxy welfare clients with or for them. The integrated services which benefit children involve publicising their private concerns among professionals. Intense health and educational surveillance exposes children to more intrusive routine examination than they will have at any other age. It is therefore especially important to distinguish essential from avoidable interference in the child's life. It will help to question in each case whether the youngster is best treated as a dependent child or, at least partly, as a competent young person.

Children's rights to own property, to work during social hours, to earn an income, to have some choice in where they live, and to make major and minor personal decisions, when they are capable of exercising such rights, have been advocated.[53] *Child-libertarians* argue that adult rights should be allowed to competent children, and insist that traditional assumptions about children's incompetence should first be justified, and not simply assumed. They are countered by *protectionists*, who believe that the state should intervene frequently in family life through education, health, and social services professionals in order to ensure high standards of child care. A third group are the *parentalists* who state that full control of the child should be left to the 'psychological parent', who is the adult in closest relationship to that particular child.[54]

Parentalists state that the parent and not the courts should define the child's best interests, and that a psychiatrist should advise the court about who the psychological parent is, since judges are not qualified to perceive who this may be. The parentalist case is criticised by lawyer John Eekelaar and sociologist Robert Dingwall on two grounds.[55] First, it is dangerously over-certain that the 'psychological parents' will not abuse their total power over the child. Second and paradoxically it is too uncertain about who the psychological parent may be. If a psychiatrist is required to divine this mysterious relationship, then its benign nature must be rather hidden and therefore perhaps unreliable. Dingwall and Eekelaar report legal cases in which judges make contradictory rulings about children's best interests. However, they conclude that disputes which reach the courts are best settled by the judges' 'common-sense psychology' which has served society for so long. Yet this does not answer the parentalists' allegation[56] that a judge's arbitrary, retrospective judgement is unjust, and that justice must entail setting clear rulings about children's interests before the event, so that parents can know when they act whether they are breaking the law. An example of a judge's arbitrary decision is the case of *In Re* R, July 1991. A girl aged 15 years and 10 months was ordered to be returned to an institution and forcibly given drugs for her episodic mental disorder. Yet in evidence, a psychiatrist had stated that the girl had decided to refuse the treatment when she was lucid and rational. The judge decided, however, within the terms of the earlier Gillick ruling, that the girl could not make an informed decision.[57]

Each view, libertarian, protectionist (by professionals) or parentalist, exposes children to risks of abuse or neglect, either by parents and other controlling adults, or by the harm which unprotected children may do to themselves, or which they may receive from others. The protective or liberal approaches apply to different stages of childhood with different emphases. Babies and dependent children benefit from protection, yet also from the liberal approach that encourages adults to listen and respond to the individual small child. Children learn to care for themselves when encouraged to make choices from an early age. In scraping away the crust of theories about childhood and its supposed inabilities, liberal views help us to see each child more clearly. They raise the key questions: *Why is the child being treated differently from adults in this case? And is the difference justified?*

Yet extreme libertarian views of society end in a chilly climate of free-floating agents, able to care for themselves and caring for others only if they choose to do so. While genuine choice is admirable it is unrealistic, since life is not so simple and small, ill or disabled children rely on consistent committed care, whatever the carers' changing views. Younger children need more protection and support than adults do. They are partly adults-in-the-making,[58] with long-term interests which they may not appreciate.

Once the forces from which children need protection are examined, many are seen to oppress adults too. Examples are the abuses and injustice in employment, in the judicial system, in the education and social services and, increasingly, the health services, which are weighted against poor, illiterate and black people. More respect for everyone's rights would also help adults, and lessen the need for special protection for children.

Determining competence

The Gillick ruling moves towards allowing children to exercise rights of decision-making when adults judge that they are competent to do so. The question shifts from 'what should adults decide for the child?' to 'when can children decide for themselves?' The literature on competence, mainly in medical decision-making, is generally conservative. It draws on psychological studies of child development, much influenced by Piaget's work in the 1930s and 1940s, and ignores the changes in children's lives since that period. Competence is usually treated as if it is a definite characteristic that can be measured like an IQ, if tests can be devised.

The work of doctors and social workers, whose decisions can so dramatically affect a child's life, would obviously be easier if they knew exactly when to stop making decisions for children, and when to respect them as competent to decide for themselves. Yet there are no simple answers. Competence develops unevenly, depending on children's ability, experiences, confidence, and relationship with their parents who reward or punish growing independence from babyhood.

The research on children's consent to surgery found that competence was variously described by hospital staff as a skill linked to maths and reading ability; cognitive reasoning; an imaginative grasp of the personal impact that a decision (about surgery) could have; independence; knowing one's own best interest's and life-plan; maturity gained through experience; and wisdom.

Some of the professionals said they had never considered that children might be competent, and one, who thought that parents should always decide, said that the concept was so worrying she had a sleepless night after her interview. Others used informal methods to assess competence, from a quick maths test or asking the child to repeat information that had been given, to fully discussing choices and their likely effects with children, or getting to know them and their family. Several adults asserted that competence, or wisdom, was too elusive and mysterious to measure.

Competence has also to be judged in context. How urgent, serious and irrevocable is the decision? How clearly and fully has the child been informed? Do the caring adults expect the child to be competent? Does the child expect or want to be responsible for the decision? Competence is invisibly affected by many social factors, such as whether the setting is peaceful, unhurried and friendly; by cultural beliefs about how dependent children should be; by adults' attitudes of respectful encouragement or contemptuous disapproval; by television role models, by changes in the law, and so on. Children's competence changes through the decades because of the effects of the changing social context.

Some professionals thought that competence could not develop until mid or late adolescence. Others believed that it could be highly developed around five-years of age, for example among children with cystic fibrosis. This condition requires daily treatment, including drugs, gruelling physiotherapy, a restricted diet, and frequent admissions to hospitals during crises. Heart-lung transplantation offers new hope, but very high risks, uncertain benefits, and a life-time of follow-up tests and drug treatment. One transplant unit admitted families for a week of assessment and intensive preparation, and a nursing sister working very closely with the children reported that she considered five-year-olds able to grasp the main issues, and make informed decisions. At the end of the week at the unit, a child's refusal would be respected, because their informed commitment to treatment was considered to be essential: 'Their life is literally in their own hands.' A few children seemed unable to understand, not because they were incapable, but because their parents (unlike most others) had not discussed with them how fatally ill they were. These children were asked to return to the unit later, if the family had found ways of sharing this knowledge.

Another transplant unit specialised in preventive care, treating children before they became unwell, instead of those who had been very ill for years and were likely to die soon. In this unit, children were not thought to be competent until early adolescence, because they had little experience of pain and illness. It was thought that, without such experience, it was hard for them to understand warnings about how they were likely to suffer during treatment, or if they did not undergo it; therefore they could not make an informed choice.

Competence is usually linked with cognitive development and progress at school, but the children with cystic fibrosis often missed school, had difficulty in concentrating, and sometimes seemed immature and cognitively delayed. Yet some people who worked closely with them saw them as wise and as having developed perceptions about death and the value of life to a level reached by few adults. It therefore seems that, if children's competence is to be understood, new ways of defining and assessing it need to be developed, and adults need to be willing to recognise emerging competence in young children.

Interviews with homeless young people in Britain show the problems which a sharp child/adult divide presents for them.[59] They talk of being treated in institutions as helpless children, and then suddenly at 16 years, or earlier if they run away, having to cope alone, without preparation or support. They need a transitional stage as young people, when they are supported yet encouraged to share in being responsible as early as possible. The interviews show how treating children as if they are competent can help to prevent misfortunes such as ending up on the streets. Children would not need to 'run away' from home or from children's homes if they had more choice in where they could live, and could move with dignity between homes. Part of their choice would be to agree to keep the rules of their chosen home. At present 'absconding' is classed as delinquency instead of as a cry for help.

Mike Lindsay, who works as a Children's Rights Officer for Leicester County Council, described how social workers wanted to place one girl in locked accommodation because she absconded. They had not asked her why she did so. The girl explained to him that she escaped because her class was doing schoolwork about their homes. She was ashamed that everyone at school would learn that she was in care. Once the matter was sorted out with her teacher she was willing to remain at the home.[60]

Treating children with respect can markedly increase their competence. A Norwegian sociologist, Ann Solberg, has done research with hundreds of 12-year-olds.[61] She found that when parents expected them to be responsible, the children responded in such adult ways that they were given more and more responsibility, and coped with it well. But children whose parents perceived them as immature remained dependent or became rebellious. Each group confirmed their parents' expectations.

Competence often seems to be as much in the eye of the beholder as in the ability of the child. How can children be encouraged to make decisions and to share in procedures affecting them, while at the same time being protected from the risks of self-determination? The lawyer Sheila McLean points out that in Scottish law children are regarded as moral agents, responsible for their misdeeds, from the age of five and therefore it would be logical to regard them as also potentially capable of deciding their best interests.[62] She suggests that children should not be assessed for their supposed overall competence. Instead the child's particular decision should be assessed on whether it is informed and sensible. Adults would then have to be more specific when arguing why the child's choice should be overruled. All advocates of extending children's rights insist that these must not be forced upon unwilling children, but made available for them to exercise if they choose. In the research on children's consent to surgery, many children choose to leave the decision to their parents or doctors.

In law children do not have adult freedom to make any choice, however dangerous or foolish. The choice must be justifiably in the child's interests, or at least not against the interests of the child. If the child disagrees with her parents or closest carers, instead of taking a parentalist or protectionist line of accepting certain adults' views, more people could be drawn into making the decision. For example, in decisions about surgery or a medical examination which the child is strongly resisting, nurses, a psychologist, social worker, therapist, teacher or chaplain may be involved. Discussion with several professionals may help to clarify how reasonable the child's objection is, how necessary the procedure, and whether it can be delayed, modified or cancelled. Through discussion young people can express fears and uncertainty, and seek reassurance. They may come to some agreement, such as, 'I don't want it but I see why I need to have it.'

As far as abused children are concerned, research suggests that we know very little about what they think and want. Investigations about child witnesses in court have concluded that very young children can recall and recount events accurately, if they are treated considerately, and that children are less likely than adults to embroider their reports.[63] Video recordings of interviews with children suspected of satanic abuse indicate that children's suggestibility is limited, and that they continue to repeat their first account, even after weeks of pressure to change it. Empirical research is challenging traditional beliefs about children's inability to understand and act reliably. Children's rights officers working with disadvantaged children emphasise the importance of respecting their wishes. It could be argued that if some adults have abused their power over children, there is even greater onus on other adults to defer to these children if possible, and to help them to learn to make their own decisions.

Major and minor decisions

Major decisions, such as whether to have an operation, frequently break down into several minor decisions – when, where, and how the patient is treated, prepared, nursed and helped during recovery, what pain relief or physiotherapy will be given, and so on. Pre-school children may be able to share in at least some of these decisions, when they are informed and consulted, even if the overall decision, such as whether to have surgery, is thought to be beyond their competence.

Although limited choice can be better than none, it is not always so. This is illustrated by a cartoon in a report on the distress of children in care at being moved from one placement to another. An adult is saying to a child, 'We're moving you – do you want to go by bus or train?'[64] If procedural rights are to be extended within the field of welfare generally and to children in particular, it is important that they are applied to decisions about major as well as minor issues. There is a danger that elaborate procedural rules will defeat their intended purpose if they mystify children and require complicated explanations. However, adults could start by giving children the benefit of the doubt. They could explore through listening (rather than through formal tests) whether children can understand much or little, and can make major or at least minor decisions, before deciding whether to exclude them from decision-making.

Rights for children and young people in a modern welfare system

Three common prejudices at present restrict society's respect for children's rights:

* children are dependent, inadequate individuals who need only protection and care;
* the state should not interfere with families unless children are neglected or abused;
* parents should be responsible for their children until they are financially independent.

To a certain extent these are embodied in the 1989 Children Act which emphasises child protection, parents' responsibilities, and local authorities' limited resources. The Act provides only a limited framework for any proposal for children's rights. In contrast, the UN Convention, when ratified and combined with the Gillick ruling, would provide a firmer basis for children's rights, founded on a different set of assumptions:

* children can be treated as sensible people who have the right to share in making decisions about their lives as soon as they are competent and wish to do so;
* the state already affects children's lives in many ways, politically and economically;
* parents are often unable to care for their children adequately because

of social structures such as poverty, unemployment, poor housing, and racism.

There is still a long way to go before standards in the UK meet those in the UN Convention.[65]

The final part of this chapter lists certain children's rights. Some are already enshrined in law, others are recommended in guidelines, and others are still contended as, slowly, the concept of children's rights becomes more widely recognised. Some rights may seem too obvious to be worth stating; they are included because they are still frequently denied to children and young people.

Procedural rights, although designed for everyone to use, are mainly for solving individual problems. They need to be complemented by regular review and improvement of practices generally. Methods which are used in other countries, and some that have been used but discontinued in the UK should be considered for this purpose: they include neighbourhood councils with child members to work for their collective interests; local children's rights officers as in Leicestershire; and family courts which are relatively informal and non-adversarial, run by lawyers and others particularly concerned about children. Proposals for children's advocacy at a national level include: a Children's Committee, re-established to advocate children's interests; restoring Ministers' annual reports to Parliament on progress and omissions in respect of children's rights, with an 'impact on children' statement about all the work of their department; a children's rights commissioner;[66] rationalising disparate laws affecting children, coordinating them and bringing them up to date.

Basic rights for all children

As set out in the United Nations Convention on the Rights of the Child, every child should have the right to:

* a standard of living adequate for the child's physical, mental and social development;
* adequate health services and preventive health care;
* a reasonably safe environment;
* adequate play areas and preschool services;
* protection from 'all forms of physical or mental violence, injury or abuse, neglect or negligent treatment, maltreatment or exploitation' from parents or other carers;
* education and care which respect the child's dignity, freedom of expression, freedom of thought and conscience, and ethnic origins;
* appropriate services for children with disabilities and special needs.

Substantive rights for all children, especially those in institutions

Practical details following from general rights have been worked out by some local authorities in the UK. For example, the Scottish region of Strathclyde has published a report, *Home or Away*, which details rights that the authority would wish to give to young people in its care. Building on this and other work, we propose that all children, and especially those in institutions, should have the right to:

* contact with their friends and family (including help with travel and telephone costs if needed);
* privacy – a place to be alone and non-interference with personal mail and telephone calls;
* space – not to be locked-up or punished without a fair trial;
* individual property and a safe place to keep it;
* a say in the purchase of personal items like clothing and food;
* a say in the running of the establishment where they live;
* due consultation before being moved to another residence.

Procedural rights

As a means to an end, procedures affect the end or outcome, by partly determining the range of options considered, who considers them, and how they are considered. Involving children in procedures is, therefore, a vital means not only of respecting them, but also of benefiting them. When children share in planning or reviewing their care, their views can be explained and attended to. They are also more likely to understand and agree with decisions which they have shared in making. During procedures, children should have as much help and advocacy as they wish but no more, with adults attempting to combine protection with respect, and support with freedom.

Young people's procedural rights apply mainly in institutions, in schools, hospitals, and for children in care and in custody. The 1989 Children Act states that children's wishes and feelings should be ascertained and attended to, and that children should make decisions when they have 'sufficient understanding to make an informed decision'. Some local authorities, such as Strathclyde, are beginning to document details.

As far as possible, children should have the right:

* to an active share in all decisions about their care;
* to read and add comments to all reports about them, however painful the information in the reports might be;
* to know the full details of their personal, family, and other relevant circumstances;

* to have help to accept the implications of this information;
* to have help in putting forward their own point of view in all forums which make decisions about their future;
* to have an interpreter, if necessary, who will repeat the discussion in the child's first language and state the child's views;
* to choose someone they trust to attend forums with them;
* to have a regular review and the right to ask for a review;
* to be informed in writing of relevant meetings, decisions, and the reasons for the decisions;
* to have access to independent, external legal advice and representation when in custody;
* to appeal against decisions by education, health or welfare agencies, or to complain, and to have the child's views formally reviewed;
* to make a further appeal to an impartial external authority.

The framework of rights for adults in other chapters would apply to young people as soon as they are old enough to be involved in personal decisions.

The future

This chapter has aimed to show that rights are more likely to reflect the interests and wishes of right holders who can choose, claim and assert them. Traditionally, children have been excluded from deciding what is in their own best interests. Changes in law and in society challenge former assumptions about children's inabilities and open the way for them to be more involved in negotiating their own rights. Authority to determine the child's interests, instead of being allocated to the parents or the professionals, should increasingly be shared between adults and children, with young children taking on more authority as they become competent young people.

NOTES

1 Citizenship, Rights and Welfare
Raymond Plant

1. The discussion of citizen's charters has tended to focus on how the issue came to be put on the agenda of the Conservative Government under Mr Major and as such has concentrated on the recent work of the Adam Smith Institute and the Institute of Economic Affairs. However, I could perhaps take this opportunity of pointing out that I argued for this kind of approach from a left wing perspective at a conference held by the IEA early in 1989 and in a series of articles in *The Times* in 1988 and 1989. The paper from the conference was published by the IEA in R. Plant and N. Barry *Citizenship and Rights in Thatcher's Britain: Two Views*, IEA, London, 1990.

2. John Gray has now changed his mind, see *Freedom, Justice and the Morality of the Market*, IEA, London, forthcoming.

3. John Gray once held this highly relativist view see 'Classical Liberalism, Positional Goods and the Politicisation Of Poverty' in A. Ellis and K. Kumar (eds), *Dilemmas of Liberal Democracies*, Tavistock, London, 1983, p.182. However, he has now retracted this view as is seen in the IEA pamphlet cited above.

2 A Social Charter for Britain
Norman Lewis and Mary Seneviratne

1. Articles 1, 5, 6, 12, 13, 16 and 19.
2. Articles 2(1), 4(3), 7(1), 7(4), 7(7), 8(2) and 8(3).
3. Article 12(1).
4. Respectively, Articles 12(2), 12(3) and 12(4).
5. Article 21.
6. Article 29.
7. Respectively, Part II, Articles 7-12; Part III, Articles 13-8; Part IV, Articles 19-24; Part V, Articles 25-30; Part VII, Articles 39-45.
8. Respectively, Parts VI, IX and X.
9. *The Constitution of the United Kingdom*, IPPR, London, 1991.
10. Ibid. See also *A British Bill of Rights*, IPPR, London, 1990.
11. Ibid, p.22.
12. This case concerned the Home Secretary's ban on broadcasting direct statements from members of the IRA. Although the House of Lords affirmed that where British legislation was ambiguous then the Convention on Human Rights could be used as an aid to interpretation, the same was not true in reviewing the exercise of a Minister's discretion.

13. Resolution 649 (1977).

14. For example, Recommendation 1103 (1989) on the future role of the Council of Europe in the process of European construction, etc.

15. In almost all instances the examples are taken from the Committee of Independent Experts Conclusions on the Reports, XI-XII, 1989.

16. Conclusion XI, p.27.

17. See in particular *Government by Moonlight: the Hybrid Parts of the State*, Birkinshaw, Harden and Lewis, Unwin Hyman, London, 1990.

18. For example, Article 13(3).

3 Procedural Rights in Social Welfare
Denis Galligan

1. *1.* For further analysis of discretion, see D.J. Galligan, *Discretionary Powers*, OUP, Oxford, 1986.

2. See J. Mashaw, *Due Process in the Administrative State*, Yale, New Haven, 1985.

3. For discussion of these issues, see D.J. Galligan, *The Foundations of Procedural Fairness* OUP, Oxford, forthcoming.

4. In a famous book, *Discretionary Justice*, Baton Rouge, 1965, K.C. Davies argued that the structuring of discretion reduces the risk of arbitrariness.

5. On the limitations of structuring, see D.J. Galligan, *Discretionary Powers*, op.cit., pp.164–83.

6. See J. Raz, 'On the Nature of Rights', xciii *Mind*, 1984, p.194.

7. For futher discussion, see R.M. Dworkin, *A Matter of Principle*, OUP, Oxford, 1985, chapter 3.

8. For analysis, see M. Bayles, *Procedural Justice*, Kluwer, 1990.

9. See Dworkin, op.cit., chapter 3.

4 Community Care: Applying Procedural Fairness
Nick Doyle and Tessa Harding

1. Chronically Sick and Disabled Persons Act 1970.

2. Disabled Persons (Services, Consultation and Representation) Act 1986.

3. Key indicators of local authority social services 1988/9, Department of Health 1990.

4. N. Pfeffer and A. Coote, *Is Quality Good For You?* IPPR, London, 1991.

5. I. Bynoe, M. Oliver and C. Barnes, *Equal Rights for Disabled People: The case for a new law*, IPPR, 1991.

5 Rights to Health and Health Care
Jonathan Montgomery

1. J. Raz, *The Morality of Freedom*, OUP, Oxford, 1986, chapter 7.

2. R. Dworkin, *Taking Rights Seriously*, Duckworth, London, 1977.

3. R. Nozick, *Anarchy, State and Utopia*, Basil Blackwell, Oxford, 1974.

4. L. Doyal and I. Gough, *A Theory of Human Need*, Macmillan, London, 1991.

5. J. Montgomery, 'Recognising a Right to Health' in R. Beddard and D. Hill, *Economic, Social and Cultural Rights: Progress and Achievement*, Macmillan, London, 1991.

6. N. Pfeffer and A. Coote, *Is Quality Good for You?*, IPPR, London, 1991.

7. G. Hunt, ' "Patient Choice" and the National Health Service Review', *Journal of Social Welfare Law*, 1990, pp.245–55.

8. World Health Organisation, *Constitution of the World Health Organisation*, WHO, Geneva 1948.

9. A. Beattie, 'Knowledge and control in health promotion: a test case for social policy and social theory' in J. Gabe, M. Calnan and M. Bury (eds), *The Sociology of the Health Service*, Routledge, London, 1991.

10. N. Daniels, 'Health care needs and distributive justice' in R. Bayer, A. Caplan, and N. Daniels (eds), *In Search of Equity: health needs and the health care system*, Hastings Center, New York, 1983.

11. T. McKeown, *The Role of Medicine*, Basil Blackwell, Oxford, 1979.

12. P. Townsend, N. Davidson and M. Whitehead (eds), *Inequalities in Health*, Penguin, London, 1988.

13. J. Montgomery, 'Victims or threats? The framing of HIV', *Liverpool Law Review*, 12, 1990, pp.25–53.

14. S. Harrison, *et al.*, *Health before Health Care*, IPPR, London, 1991, p.6.

15. N. Rose, 'Unreasonable rights: mental illness and the limits of the law', 12, *Journal of Law and Society*, 1985, pp.199–218.

16. J. Montgomery, 'Power over death: the final sting' in D. Morgan, and R. Lee (eds) *Deathduties: law and ethics at the ending of life*, Routledge, London, 1992, forthcoming.

17. This overrules suggestions to the contrary in *Re R* [1991] 4 All ER 177 and affirms the position established in *Gillick v W. Norfolk & Wisbech AHA* [1985] 3 All ER 402.

18. See for example, A. Capron, 'A National Commission on Medical Ethics?' in P. Byrne (ed.), *Health, Rights and Resources*, Kings Fund, London, 1988.

19. J.M. Jacob, *Doctors and Rules*, Routledge, London, 1988, pp.156–68.

20. A. Simanowitz, 'Medical accidents: the problem and the challenge' in P. Byrne (ed.), *Medicine in Contemporary Society*, Kings Fund, London, 1987.

21. J. Montgomery, 'Medicine, accountability and professionalism', *Journal of Law and Society*, 16, 1989, pp.319–39.

22. S. McLean, 'No fault liability and medical responsibility' in M.D.A. Freeman, *Medicine, Ethics and the Law*, Stevens, London, 1988.

6 Rights and Social Work
Nina Biehal, Mike Fisher, Peter Marsh, Eric Sainsbury

1. A. Walker, 'Managing the package of care: implications for the user', in I. Allen (ed.), *Social Services Departments as Managing Agencies*, Policy Studies Institute, London, 1989.

2. D. Taylor, 'Citizenship and social power', *Critical Social Policy*, 1989, 9, 2, pp.19–31.

3. R. Bhaduri, 'Race and culture: the "invisible" consumers', in I. Allen (ed.), *Hearing the Voice of the Consumer*, Policy Studies Institute, London, 1988.

4. A. Bebbington and H. Charnley, 'Community care for the elderly – rhetoric or reality', *British Journal of Social Work*, 20, 1990, pp.409–32.

5. P. Taylor-Gooby, 'Needs, welfare and political allegiance', in N. Timms (ed.), *Social Welfare: Why and How?*, Routledge and Kegan Paul, London, 1980.

6. J. Neill, I. Sinclair, P. Gorbach and J. Williams, *A Need for Care: A Study of Elderly Applicants for Local Authority Residential Care*, Avebury, Aldershot, 1988.

7. M. Barnes, R. Bowl and M. Fisher, *Sectioned: Social Services and the Mental Health Act 1983*, Routledge, London, 1990.

8. W. Reid and P. Hanrahan, 'The effectiveness of social work: recent evidence', in E. Goldberg and N. Connelly (eds), *Evaluative Research in Social Care*, Heinemann Educational Books, London, 1981, pp.9–20.

9. P. Marsh 'Researching practice and practising research in child care social work', in M. Fisher (ed.), *Speaking of Clients*, Joint Unit for Social Services Research, University of Sheffield, Sheffield, pp.47–59.

10. British Association of Social Workers, *Clients are Fellow Citizens – Report of the Working Party on Client Participation in Social Work*, British Association of Social Workers, Birmingham, 1980.

11. National Council for Voluntary Organisations, *Clients' Rights*, Bedford Square Press, London, 1984.

12. Wagner Committee *Residential Care: A Positive Choice*, HMSO, London, 1988.

13. Department of Health and Social Security (1983) Circular LAC (83), *Personal Social Services Records*, HMSO, London.

14. D. Gay and W. Fox, 'Open to reason?', *Insight*, 6 December 1988, pp.12–15.

15. Department of Health and Social Security, *Code of Practice – Access to Children in Care*, HMSO, London, 1983.

16. D. Howe, *An Introduction to Social Work Theory*, Wildwood House, Aldershot, 1987.

17. P. Marsh, 'Changing practice in child care – the Children Act 1989', *Adoption and Fostering*, 14, 4, 1990, pp.27–30.

18. R. Parker, *Safeguarding Standards*, National Institute for Social Work, London, 1990.

7 Realising Rights Through Local Service Contracts
Wendy Thomson

1. A. Bartholomew, 'Should a Marxist Believe in Marx on Rights?', in Miliband and Panitch (eds), *The Retreat of the Intellectuals, Socialist Register*, 1990, Merlin Press, London.

2. Labour Party, *The Charter of Rights*, 1991. See also, Labour Party, Quality Commission, 1991; Labour Party, *Quality Street*, 1989.

3. T. Jowell, 'Our Common Agenda', *The Ditchley Report*, The Joseph Rowntree Foundation's Prospectus for Community Care, 1991.

8 Rights of Children and Young People
Priscilla Alderson

1. *Gillick v. West Norfolk and Wisbeach AHA*, 1985, 3 All ER 402.

2. Lord Denning in *Hewer v. Bryant*, 969, 3 All ER 578.

3. United Nations, *Convention on the Rights of the Child*, 1989, articles, 13, 14, 15.

4. UN Convention, article 12.

5. UN Convention, article 41.

6. *L'Observatatore Romano*, 28 November 1989, p.12.

7. A. Miller, *For your own good: the roots of violence in child-rearing*, Virago, London, 1980.

8. By philosophers such as M. Tooley, J. Harris and P. Sionger.

9. F. Frohock, *Special care*, University of Chicago Press, Chicago, 1986, R. Stinson and P. Stinson, *The long dying of baby Andrew*, Little Brown, Boston, 1983.

10. A. Coote, H. Harman and P. Hewitt, *The Family Way: A new approach to policy-making*, IPPR, London, 1990.

11. UN Convention on the Rights of the Child 1989, article 1.

12. The Children's Legal Centre published regular summaries of age-based legislation, see *Childright*, 73:11–14, 1991.

13. J. Hughes, 'Thinking about children', in G. Scarre (ed.), *Children, parents and politics*, CUP, Cambridge, 1989, pp.36–51.

14. P. Alderson, *Children's consent to surgery*, report on a research project, 1989-91. 120 people aged 8-15 years having orthopaedic surgery, and the adults caring for them, were interviewed in four hospitals, Open University Press, forthcoming.

15. J. Piaget, B. Inhelder, *The child's conception of space*, Routledge & Kegan Paul, London, 1956.

16. L. Kohlberg, *The Philosophy of moral development*, Harper & Row, New York, 1981.

17. M. Donaldson, *Children's minds*, Fontana, Edinburgh, 1978.

18. C. Gilligan, *In a different voice*, Harvard University Press, Cambridge, Mass., 1982.

19. J. Holt, *Escape from Childhood*, Penguin, Harmondsworth, 1975.

20. J. Kitzinger, 'Who are you kidding? Children, power and the struggle against sexual abuse', in A. James and A. Prout (eds), *Constructing and reconstructing childhood: new directions in the sociological study of childhood*, Falmer Press, Basingstoke, 1990, pp.157–83.

21. P. Newell, *Children are people too: the case against physical punishment*, Bedford Square Press, London, 1989, p.25.

22. National Children's Home, *Left to their own devices: a report on youth homelessness*, London, 1990.

23. Child Accident Prevention Trust Report, *Safe as houses*, London, 1991.

24. Bandana Ahmed, in *Working together for children's welfare, partnership and the Children Act 1989*, conference report, Michael Sieff Foundation, Surrey, 1990.

25. Widely discussed, for example in the Scottish Law Commission's discussion paper no.75, *The evidence of children and other potentially vulnerable witnesses*, June 1988, and the Commission's research paper on proceedings in the USA, *Evidence from children*, K. Murray, 1988.

26. National Children's Bureau intervention research project 1988-91, 'Who says?': enabling children to participate in planning and decision making, reported in R. Gardner, 'Who says?' choice and control in care, NCB, London, 1987.

27. See note 14.

28. M. Cheitlin (ed.), *Dilemmas in clinical cardiology*, Davis, Philadelphia, 1990. Cheitlin's remark referred to one therapy, but a reviewer commented that 'best guess' could apply throughout the book, anon., *British Medical Journal*, 302:541, 1991.

29. Pet Animals Act 1951, sect.3.

30. S. Lukes, *Power: a radical view*, Basingstoke, Macmillan, 1974.

31. M. Woodhead, 'Psychology and cultural construction of children's needs', in James and Prout, op.cit. See note 22, 60–77.

32. United Nations, *Convention on the Rights of the Child*, 1989.

33. J. Locke, *Two treatises of civil government*, Dent, London, 1924.

34. I. Kant, *Groundwork of the metaphysic of morals*, Hutchinson, London, 1948.

35. J. Grimshaw, *Feminist philosophers*, Wheatsheaf, Brighton, 1986, analyses sexism in rights philosophy.

36. See note 8.

37. See note 13.

38. V. Seidler, *Kant, respect and injustice*, Routledge and Kegan Paul, London, 1986.

39. P. Alderson, Children's consent project (see note 14) and *Choosing for children: parents' consent to surgery*, OUP, Oxford, 1990, shows how adults learn through emotions.

40. The spirit of the Convention is summarised in these words in K. Castells, *In the child's best interest: a primer on the UN Convention on the Rights of the Child, 1989*, Foster Parents Plan International, London.

41. See note 32.

42. See note 32, article 37. The right is better expressed in article 19, quoted later.

43. J. Eekelaar, 'The emergence of children's rights' *Oxford Journal of Legal Studies*, 6, 2:161–82, 1986.

44. Low Pay Unit and Birmingham City Council, *Hidden Army*, a report on child employment, 1991.

45. R. Franklin (ed.), *The rights of children*, Oxford, Blackwell, 1986.

46. Court Report *Fit for the future: report of the committee on child health services*, London, HMSO, 1976.

47. *The report of the committee of enquiry into the education of handicapped children and young persons* (Warnock Report), London, HMSO, 1978.

48. United Nations Charter of Rights, 1948, article 25.

49. N. Rose, *Governing the soul: the shaping of the private self*, London, Routledge, 1990.

50. Katharine Mansfield, quoted at the start of the *Court Report*, ref. 54.

51. J. Eekelaar, 'The emergence of children's rights', *Oxford Journal of Legal Studies*, 6, 2: pp.161–82, 1986.

52. B. Mayall and M.C. Foster, *Child health care*, Heinemann, London, 1989.

53. R. Farson, *Birthrights*, Penguin, Harmondsworth, 1978; J. Holt, *Escape from Childhood*, Penguin, Harmondsworth, 1975.

54. J. Goldstein, A. Freud and A. Solnit, *Beyond the best interests of the child*, 1973, and *Before the best interests of the child*, Burnett Books, New York, 1979.

55. R. Dingwall and J. Eekelaar, 'Judgements of Solomon: psychology and family law', in *Children of social worlds*, M. Richards and P. Light (eds), Harvard University Press, Cambridge, Mass., 1986.

56. See note 61.

57. 'In *Re R.*, a minor', *The Times*, 31 July 1991.

58. A. Buchanan and D. Brock, *Deciding for others*, CUP, New York, 1989; G. Melton, G. Koocher, and M. Saks (eds), *Children's competence to consent*, Plenum Press, New York, 1983; W. Gaylin and R. Macklin, *Who speaks for the child*? Plenum Press, New York, 1982; the section on 'children's and parents' roles in medical decision making' in L.

Kopelman and J. Moskop (eds), *Children and health care: moral and social issues*, Kluwer, Dordecht, 1989.

59. See note 22.

60. 'Getting it right for children in care', *Children first*, UNICEF Journal, London, Autumn 1990, p.19.

61. A. Solberg, 'Negotiating childhood' in James and Prout (eds), see note 20.

62. S. McLean, *A patient's right to know*, Dartmouth, Aldershot, 1989.

63. King and Yuille 1987, quoted in J. Spencer and R. Flin, *The evidence of children: the law and psychology*, Blackstone Press, London, 1990; *Report of the advisory group on video evidence*, Home Office, 1989.

64. R. Gardner, *Who says? choice and control in care*, National Children's Bureau, 1987.

65. P. Newell, *The UN Convention and Children's Rights*, National Children's Bureau, London, 1991.

66. The case is clearly argued in M. Rosenbaum and P. Newell, *Taking children seriously: a proposal for a children's Rights Commissioner*, Calouste Gulbenkian Foundation, London, 1991.